SpringerBriefs in Psychology

Best Practices in Cognitive-Behavioral Psychotherapy

Epidemiological studies show that the prevalence of mental disorders is extremely high across the globe (World Health Organization, 2011). Moreover, and what is perhaps more concerning is the fact that, despite numerous existing evidence-based treatments for various mental disorders, more than half of those in need of specialized mental health services don't access it and/or do not have access to these treatments (Alonso et al., 2004c; Kohn, Saxena, Levav, & Saraceno, 2004; Wang et al., 2005). Thus, developing and disseminating accessible evidence-based protocols for various clinical conditions are key goals in mental health. This effort would nicely complement the efforts of the American Psychological Association (see Division 12's List of evidence-based treatments), National Institute for Health and Clinical Excellence (see NICE's Guidelines) and Cochrane Reviews (see Cochrane analyses of various clinical protocols) that identified evidence-based treatments for various clinical conditions, based on rigorous literature analyses. However, once identified, one needs a detailed published clinical protocol to deliver those treatments in research, clinical practice, and/or training (see David & Montgomery, 2011). Please submit your proposal to Series Editor Daniel David: daniel.david@ubbcluj.ro

More information about this series at http://www.springer.com/series/10143

Cezar Giosan

Cognitive Evolutionary Therapy for Depression

Therapy Manual

Springer

Cezar Giosan
Department of Psychology
University of Bucharest
Bucharest, Romania

ISSN 2365-077X ISSN 2365-0788 (electronic)
Best Practices in Cognitive-Behavioral Psychotherapy
ISSN 2192-8363 ISSN 2192-8371 (electronic)
SpringerBriefs in Psychology
ISBN 978-3-030-38873-7 ISBN 978-3-030-38874-4 (eBook)
https://doi.org/10.1007/978-3-030-38874-4

This Springer imprint is published by the registered company Springer Nature Switzerland AG
The registered company address is: Gewerbestrasse 11, 6330 Cham, Switzerland

Acknowledgments

The author would like to thank Vlad Mureşan, Oana Cobeanu, Cristina Mogoaşe, Aurora Szentagotai, and Alina Rusu for their inputs and comments on the various iterations of this manuscript.

Also, special thanks to David Buss, Todd Shackelford, and Aurelio Jose Figueredo for their valuable help and early feedback on this work.

Note: This work was supported by a UEFISCDI grant awarded to Cezar Giosan through the Department of Clinical Psychology and Psychotherapy, Babeş-Bolyai University, Cluj-Napoca, Romania.

Contents

Chapter 1
Evolutionary Psychology – A Brief Introduction

In the distant future I see open fields for far more important researches. Psychology will be based on a new foundation, that of the necessary acquirement of each mental power and capacity by gradation.

Charles Darwin, The Origin of Species, 1859

Little did Charles Darwin know, a century and a half ago, that his prophetic words would constitute the foundation of a modern discipline within the broad field of psychology, namely "Evolutionary Psychology." Evolutionary psychology examines psychological traits and processes – such as memory, perception, or language – from a modern evolutionary perspective (Buss, 2005). It seeks to identify which (typically human) psychological traits and mechanisms are adaptations, that is, the functional products of natural selection. The approach is similar to that in medicine, wherein organs (e.g., heart, liver) are understood in the context of the survival and reproductive functions they serve. Although a relatively new development in psychology, significant progress has been made in the field in the past two decades. Behaviors that could not be explained well before, such as the causes of gender differences in sexual preferences, or altruistic behavior towards kin, have received ultimate-cause explanations deriving from the insights of evolutionary psychology (Buss, 2005).

Evolutionary psychology uses an adaptationist approach to understand and explain cognitive structures and argues that different "pieces" of our cognitive system serve different adaptive functions, which are related to recurrent adaptive problems that humans faced in the ancestral environments (Buss, 2005; Confer et al., 2010). Evolutionary psychology is not just a sub-discipline of psychology, but a foundational framework that integrates and reinterprets the entire field of psychology, in a similar way that Darwinism has done for biology (Cosmides, 1997; Ploeger, van der Maas, & Raijmakers, 2008).

While the classical approach in psychology, known as the "standard social science model" (Cosmides, 1997), has historically considered the human cognitive

C. Giosan, *Cognitive Evolutionary Therapy for Depression*, SpringerBriefs in Psychology, https://doi.org/10.1007/978-3-030-38874-4_1

system to include abstract processes and general-problem solving domains, such as reasoning and decision making, evolutionary psychologists describe evolved psychological mechanisms as narrowly focused to deal with specific problems, such as cheaters detection, mate selection, incest avoidance, or parental investment (Kurzban, 2011). Evolutionary psychology views the human brain as being comprised of many such functional mechanisms, called *psychological adaptations*, which are the results of natural selection (Barkow, Cosmides, & Tooby, 1995; Kurzban, 2011).

As with adaptations in general, psychological adaptations are intrinsically related to the specific environment in which they evolved, termed *the Environment of Evolutionary Adaptedness, or the EEA* (Tooby & Cosmides, 1990). The EEA is not a specific point/place in time, but rather a collection of historically recurring selection pressures that led to an adaptation through natural selection.

1.1 The Environment of Evolutionary Adaptedness

Humans, comprising the genus *Homo*, appeared between 1.5 and 2.5 million years ago, a time that coincides with the start of the Pleistocene about 1.8 million years ago. Because the Pleistocene ended a mere 12,000 years ago, coinciding roughly with the discovery of agriculture (about 10,000 years ago), most human adaptations evolved before or during that period, which, for us, represents the Environment of Evolutionary Adaptedness. Evolutionary psychologists therefore argue that the majority of human cognitive modules are adapted to reproductive and survival problems frequently encountered in the Pleistocene environments (Barkow et al., 1995). In broad terms, these problems include those of growth, development, differentiation, maintenance, mating, parenting, and social relationships. The argument that our species is adapted to pre-agricultural environments becomes even stronger when we factor in the fact that, just 5000 years ago, only half of the population had fully transitioned to agriculture.

Since our adaptations are suited to the ancestral environments we evolved in as a species, a novel and different environment can result in a mismatch between it and our psychological mechanisms (Irons, 1998). Such mismatches can explain many psychological phenomena and we will mention here just one example: humans develop phobias of ancestral threats (e.g., snakes, insects, or heights) with relative ease, but they rarely develop phobias of modern, far more dangerous inventions, which were not present in the ancestral environments (e.g., pollution, cigarettes, guns, traffic, or driving) (Pinker, 2009).

The Pleistocene climate was characterized by repeated glacial cycles, during which up to 30% of the planet's surface was covered with ice, stretching to North America, Northern Europe, and even New Zealand. Because these periods were characterized by severe lack of food, many extremely large mammals (e.g., the mammoths) went extinct during that time. Another important casualty of those harsh conditions were the Neanderthals, who disappeared around 40,000 years ago.

The modern humans – Homo Sapiens – appeared in Africa about 300,000 years ago and began to migrate approximately 100,000–70,000 years ago, passing through what is nowadays Ethiopia and Yemen, populating Australia, Asia and Europe, and, eventually, crossing the Bering strait and ending with the migration in the Americas, about 20,000 years ago.

Before settling down in the post-agricultural, permanent dwellings, about 10,000–5000 years ago, humans lived in groups of hunter-gatherers, who migrated frequently in search for better conditions and resources. Men were the hunters, their main responsibility being, besides protection, to provide protein for their kin. They traveled far distances hunting game, often venturing into unfamiliar, potentially dangerous territories. It was, therefore, vital for them to be able to find their way back, which made them evolve good mapping skills. Women, on the other hand, supplied the role of gatherers, collecting edible foods from the surroundings, such as berries, vegetables, nuts, or sprouts. Since for women, unlike men, the sources of food did not change location from one minute to another (antelopes move around, but banana trees do not), women should have slowly evolved better memory than men for the localization of static objects. This gender difference in cognitive abilities, with women showing better memory for object location, has been confirmed by studies in cognitive psychology (Silverman, Choi, & Peters, 2007).

The most common misconception why women assumed the role of gatherers and not hunters is that men generally have stronger physiques. In fact, the reason why women evolved to be the gatherers had more to do with pregnancy and motherhood and less with a difference in physical abilities. When women do hunt, they can be at least as successful as men. For example, in the Aeta tribe from the Philippines, the majority of women are hunters, hunting the same animals as men. They use dogs and have a success rate of about 30% in comparison with men, who have a success rate of only about 18% (Dahlberg, 1983).

Hunter-gatherer societies subsisted on hunting, fishing, foraging, and, occasionally scavenging. During our pre-agricultural times, our species did not consume milk (other than newborns consuming mother's milk), which explains the fact that a substantial proportion of people nowadays have lactose intolerance (NIH, n.d.). Archeological data also show that, after the transition to grains, our species faced serious health issues, such as lack of vitamins and dental and bones problems, due to a sharp reduction in the vital nutrients typically found in the diet of the hunter-gatherers.

Socially, our ancestors lived in migratory groups of about 150 people, rarely more than 300. This number – 150 – is known as the Dunbar number, which represents a cognitive limit to the number of people with whom one can maintain stable social relationships (Dunbar, 1992). Dunbar arrived at this conclusion well before the advent of social networking sites, by analyzing the number of postcards people sent on Christmas. Although the investment was minimal, in general people did not send postcards to more than about 150 people, out of whom about a quarter were relatives, two thirds were friends, and the rest were colleagues (Bennett, 2013). Dunbar argues that this cognitive limit influences many aspects of our lives. For instance, the hunter-gatherer tribes still existing nowadays number about 150 members; The smallest military units typically consist of 80–150 people; Most groups split when their members are more than 150.

The tribal hunter-gatherer societies from the Pleistocene consisted of young men and women, as well as children. In many such tribes there were older people as well, but their number was a lot smaller than that in the modern societies (Gurven & Kaplan, 2007). But how do we know that this lifestyle characterized our ancestors the way we describe? Absent a time-travel machine, we base our conclusions on anthropological evidence, and, crucially, on observations of the hunter-gatherer societies still existing today. The San Bushmen from the Kalahari desert, or the hunter-gatherer tribes in Tanzania (e.g., the Hadza people) or Papua New Guinea, or the hunter-gatherers living in the Amazonian forest, offer an extraordinary window into the lives of our ancestors (Marlowe, 2005).

In these groups, women have in general the same status as men do, hunter-gatherer societies being much more egalitarian than many modern societies, including the United States. The fact that hunter-gatherers function within such norms is even more extraordinary when we think that our closest relatives – the chimpanzees – are structured hierarchically, with an all-powerful alpha male on top.

During the Environment of Evolutionary Adaptedness, tribal societies faced a series of major threats to survival. Lack of food was likely the greatest challenge. It pushed our species out of Africa and made us adapt to long stretches of time (as many as several weeks) without food. An immediate and obvious consequence of our adaptation to starvation represents the high rates of obesity in the industrialized societies, which are about 30% in the United States. When we add the percentage of people who are overweight, this number increases to a staggering 60% (National Institutes of Health, 2012). The explanation of this phenomenon again lies in the characteristics of the EEA, which we evolved adaptations to: Our ancestors used to consume all the food that they came across, because they were never sure if they had access to food the following day. Today, the same instinct operates even when food is aplenty, which is the case in all industrialized societies, prompting us, unconsciously, to consume many more calories than we optimally need. Normally, we do not need more than about 2000–2500 calories per day to function efficiently in the modern world (Nordqvist, 2016), but our caloric intake is a lot higher (Peppers, 2014). Combined with our sedentary lifestyles, this is a recipe for a plethora of medical problems, such as diabetes and heart disease.

Evolutionary pressures made us prefer certain types of foods and tastes. In the cold climates from the Pleistocene, it helped us to consume foods rich in calories, such as fats. This preference is still linked to survival in certain nomadic populations (Badarch & Zilinskas, 2015), but in the modern environments it has become maladaptive, being associated with Syndrome X and lower life expectancy. In the same manner, we evolved preferences for sweets (e.g., ripe fruits), because they contain important nutrients. In the modern world, however, this preference makes us consume unhealthy quantities of sweets and processed sugars, which are linked to countless medical problems in both children and adults.

Unsurprisingly, populations who do consume the type of foods that we evolved adaptations to (e.g., fish, game, plenty of fruits and vegetables, nuts, eggs, occasionally honey) generally experience excellent health (Cordain, 2011; Cordain et al., 2005; O'Keefe & Cordain, 2004). Cardiovascular diseases are almost inexistent in the hunter-gatherer societies alive today. When such populations begin to consume the modern foods, they typically experience poor health outcomes. For instance, in the Maya populations in Central America, diabetes was virtually non-existent until the middle of the last century, when they transitioned to the modern foods (Gibbons, 2013).

Hunter-gatherers typically spend a lot less time "working" (i.e., searching for food), compared to modern societies. They work for about six or fewer hours per day while, in the contemporary world, the average is almost nine hours.

Group members in these hunter-gatherer societies spend almost their entire time together. Generally, they start their activity (e.g., hunting or gathering) later in the morning and finish it mid-afternoon. They are very active, walking long distances daily (about 15 km) and share their food with the rest of the group. They take many breaks and socialize almost permanently. The fact that, for almost our entire history, we spent less time working than we do today explains the results in many studies in industrial or cognitive psychology that show that our capacity to focus lasts for several hours, after which time decreases sharply, needing a break to come back (Schwartz, 2013). Looking at this through the lenses of evolution, such results are not at all surprising. We simply lack the cognitive mechanisms necessary to focus for long periods of time, because hunting or gathering were never continuous activities. On the contrary, they took place with many intermittent breaks.

References

Badarch, D., & Zilinskas, R. A. (2015). *Mongolia today: Science, culture, environment and development*. London, UK: Routledge.

Barkow, J. H., Cosmides, L., & Tooby, J. (Eds.). (1995). *The adapted mind: Evolutionary psychology and the generation of culture*. New York, NY: Oxford University Press.

Bennett, D. (2013). *The Dunbar number, from the guru of social networks*. Retrieved November 16, 2015, from BloombergView website: http://www.bloomberg.com/bw/articles/2013-01-10/the-dunbar-number-from-the-guru-of-social-networks

Buss, D. M. (2005). *The handbook of evolutionary psychology*. Hoboken, NJ: Wiley.

Confer, J. C., Easton, J. A., Fleischman, D. S., Goetz, C. D., Lewis, D. M., Perilloux, C., & Buss, D. M. (2010). Evolutionary psychology. Controversies, questions, prospects, and limitations. *The American Psychologist*, *65*(2), 110–126. https://doi.org/Review

Cordain, L. (2011). *The paleo diet: Lose weight and get healthy by eating the foods you were designed to eat* (Rev. ed). Hoboken, NJ: Wiley.

Cordain, L., Eaton, S. B., Sebastian, A., Mann, N., Lindeberg, S., Watkins, B. A., … Brand-Miller, J. (2005). Origins and evolution of the Western diet: Health implications for the 21st century. *The American Journal of Clinical Nutrition, 81*(2), 341–354.

Cosmides, L. T. J. (1997). *Evolutionary psychology: A primer*. Retrieved from http://cogweb.ucla.edu/ep/EP-primer.html

Dahlberg, F. (Ed.). (1983). *Woman the gatherer* (New ed.). New Haven, CT: Yale University Press.

Dunbar, R. I. (1992). Neocortex size as a constraint on group size in primates. *Journal of Human Evolution, 22*(6), 469–493.

Gibbons, A. (2013). *The evolution of diet*. Retrieved January 13, 2016, from National Geographic website: http://www.nationalgeographic.com/foodfeatures/evolution-of-diet/

Gurven, M., & Kaplan, H. (2007). Longevity among hunter- gatherers: A cross-cultural examination. *Population and Development Review, 33*(2), 321–365. https://doi.org/10.1111/j.1728-4457.2007.00171.x

Irons, W. (1998). Adaptively relevant environments versus the environment of evolutionary adaptedness. *Evolutionary Anthropology: Issues, News, and Reviews, 6*(6), 194–204. https://doi.org/10.1002/(SICI)1520-6505(1998)6:6<194::AID-EVAN2>3.0.CO;2-B

Kurzban, R. (2011). *Why everyone (else) is a hypocrite: Evolution and the modular mind.* Princeton, NJ: Princeton University Press.

Marlowe, F. W. (2005). Hunter-gatherers and human evolution. *Evolutionary Anthropology: Issues, News, and Reviews, 14*(2), 54–67. https://doi.org/10.1002/evan.20046

National Institutes of Health. (2012). *Overweight and obesity statistics*. Retrieved January 13, 2016, from http://www.niddk.nih.gov/health-information/health-statistics/Pages/overweight-obesity-statistics.aspx

NIH, G. H. (n.d.). *Lactose intolerance*. Retrieved February 18, 2018, from NIH.gov website: https://ghr.nlm.nih.gov/condition/lactose-intolerance

Nordqvist, C. (2016). *How many calories should I eat a day?* Retrieved January 13, 2016, from Medical News Today website: http://www.medicalnewstoday.com/articles/245588.php

O'Keefe, J. H., & Cordain, L. (2004). Cardiovascular disease resulting from a diet and lifestyle at odds with our Paleolithic genome: How to become a 21st-century hunter-gatherer. *Mayo Clinic Proceedings Mayo Clinic, 79*(1), 101–108.

Peppers, M. (2014). *America's daily calorie intake is 3,770, the highest in the world*. Retrieved January 13, 2016, from Daily Mail Online website: http://www.dailymail.co.uk/femail/article-2722815/Daily-calorie-intake-countries-world-revealed-surprise-U-S-tops-list-3-770.html

Pinker, S. (2009). *How the mind works*. Retrieved from http://books.google.com/books?id=5cXKQUh6bVQC

Ploeger, A., van der Maas, H. L. J., & Raijmakers, M. E. J. (2008). Is evolutionary psychology a metatheory for psychology? A discussion of four major issues in psychology from an evolutionary developmental perspective. *Psychological Inquiry, 19*(1), 1–18. https://doi.org/10.1080/10478400701774006

Schwartz, T. (2013, February 9). Relax! you'll be more productive. *The New York Times*. Retrieved from http://www.nytimes.com/2013/02/10/opinion/sunday/relax-youll-be-more-productive.html

Silverman, I., Choi, J., & Peters, M. (2007). The hunter-gatherer theory of sex differences in spatial abilities: Data from 40 countries. *Archives of Sexual Behavior, 36*(2), 261–268. https://doi.org/10.1007/s10508-006-9168-6

Tooby, J., & Cosmides, L. (1990). The past explains the present: Emotional adaptations and the structure of ancestral environments. *Ethology and Sociobiology, 11*, 375–424.

Chapter 2
The Concept of Fitness in Evolutionary Psychology

2.1 Definitions

Fitness, a fundamental concept in evolutionary biology, is defined as *reproductive success/number of offspring* (Fagerstrom, 1992; Fisher, 1958; Rosenberg, 1983; Sober, 1993), or as *adaptedness*, that is, properties and capacities that make an organism more adapted to the environment (Burns, 1992; Dennett, 1995; Dobzhansky, 1969; Lennox, 1991; Michod, 1999; Pianka, 1978).

For a significant period after Darwin's monumental work, it was generally believed that an organism could achieve fitness solely through the maximum number of viable offspring. This approach made it difficult to explain phenomena such as altruistic behavior, or particularly extreme altruism such as self-sacrifice, which Darwin himself saw as a threat to his theory of evolution. In 1964, however, William D. Hamilton noted that an organism can achieve success not only through direct reproduction, but also through indirect reproduction, by investing in organisms that carry copies of his or her genes – such as when a woman invests in her nephews. Hamilton proposed the concept of *inclusive fitness*, emphasizing a "gene's-eye" view of evolution (Hamilton, 1964). Thus, an organism's *inclusive fitness* is the sum of its classical fitness (how many of its own offspring it produces) and the number of equivalents of its own offspring it can add by supporting others. Other authors, such as Robert Trivers (1971), expanded on Hamilton's work by arguing that altruism towards *non-kin* evolved because it can be beneficial to an organism's fitness, much in the same way like a tit-for-tat strategy.

C. Giosan, *Cognitive Evolutionary Therapy for Depression*, SpringerBriefs in Psychology, https://doi.org/10.1007/978-3-030-38874-4_2

2.2 Evaluating Fitness

There are multiple ways by which an organism achieves fitness. According to Life History Theory (Bogaert & Rushton, 1989; Figueredo et al., 2006; MacArthur & Wilson, 1967; Pianka, 1970), an organism's available resources are finite, which translates into trade-offs in resource allocation for solving various fitness-relevant tasks. For instance, an individual can allocate resources for somatic effort (e.g., growing a larger body), or reproductive effort (pursuing mates or investing in offspring).

The extremes of these fundamental dimensions of reproduction are captured by the r/K theory. A "K-selection" strategy produces a smaller number of "fitter" offspring with higher chances of survival, whereas an "r-selection" strategy will produce a larger number of offspring, of whom only a minority may survive (Bogaert & Rushton, 1989; Figueredo et al., 2006).

When applied to humans, Life History strategy is referred to as "differential K" (Rushton, 1985), which is a continuum between a high-K and a low-K reproductive strategy. A high-K strategy in humans is theorized as a cohesive fitness strategy, in which the individual invests in somatic and parental effort to produce a fewer number of "fitter" and more competitive offspring. Traits associated with a high-K strategy are long-term thinking and planning, commitment to long-term relationships, extensive parental investment, existence of social support structures, adherence to social rules (e.g., altruism and cooperation) and careful consideration of risks (Figueredo, Vásquez, Brumbach, & Schneider, 2005; Figueredo et al., 2006; Giosan, 2006). Figueredo et al. (2005) showed that a high-K strategy is associated with personality traits typically associated with social success (high conscientiousness, extroversion, and agreeableness, and low neuroticism) while other authors showed that the same strategy is negatively correlated with a cluster of socially undesirable behaviors and positively correlated with impulse control (Wenner, Figueredo, & Jacobs, 2005).

Some Life History measures include (1) the Mini-K (Figueredo et al., 2006) and (2) the High-K Strategy Scale – HKSS (Giosan, 2006). Scores on the HKSS and the Mini-K are highly correlated with one another and with a general personality factor, thereby representing better measures of Life History strategies than alternative proxy variables (Dunkel & Decker, 2010).

Some researchers have pointed out, however, that the differential K distinction in humans may be questionable (Ellis, Figueredo, Brumbach, & Schlomer, 2009; Rowe, Vazsonyi, & Figueredo, 1997; Woodley et al., 2017), with some proposing a measure of overall fitness conceptualized as a deep level construct upon which various reproductive strategies can be used (Giosan, Wyka, Mogoașe, Cobeanu, & Szentagotai, 2018). This measure, named the *Evolutionary Fitness Scale* (EFS) (Giosan et al., 2018) is an important element in the therapy protocol proposed in this manual, and will be detailed in the next sections.

References

Bogaert, A. F., & Rushton, J. P. (1989). Sexuality, delinquency and r/K reproductive strategies: Data from a Canadian university sample. *Personality and Individual Differences, 10*, 1071–1077.

Burns, T. P. (1992). Adaptedness, evolution and a hierarchical concept of fitness. *Journal of Theoretical Biology, 154*(2), 219–237. https://doi.org/10.1016/S0022-5193(05)80404-7

Dennett, D. C. (1995). *Darwin's dangerous idea: Evolution and the meanings of life*. New York, NY: Simon and Schuster.

Dobzhansky, T. (1969). On Cartesian and Darwinian aspects of biology. In *Philosophy, science and method* (pp. 165–178). New York, NY: S. Martin's Press.

Dunkel, C., & Decker, M. (2010). Convergent validity of measures of Life-History strategy. *Personality and Individual Differences, 48*, 681–684.

Ellis, B. J., Figueredo, A. J., Brumbach, B. H., & Schlomer, G. L. (2009). Fundamental dimensions of environmental risk. *Human Nature, 20*(2), 204–268. https://doi.org/10.1007/s12110-009-9063-7

Fagerstrom. (1992). The meristem-meristem cycle as a basis for defining fitness in clonal plants. *Oikos, 63*(3), 449–453. https://doi.org/10.2307/3544971

Figueredo, A. J., Vásquez, G., Brumbach, B. H., & Schneider, S. M. R. (2005). The K-factor, covitality, and personality: A psychometric test of Life History Theory. *Human Nature, 18*, 47–73.

Figueredo, A. J., Vasquez, G., Brumbach, B. H., Schneider, S. M. R., Sefcek, J. A., Tal, I. R., … Jacobs, W. J. (2006). Consilience and Life History Theory: From genes to brain to reproductive strategy. *Developmental Review, 26*, 243–275.

Fisher, R. A. (1958). *The genetical theory of natural selection*. New York, NY: Dover.

Giosan, C. (2006). High-K Strategy Scale: A measure of the High-K independent criterion of fitness. *Evolutionary Psychology, 4*, 394–405.

Giosan, C., Wyka, K., Mogoaşe, C., Cobeanu, O., & Szentagotai, A. (2018). The Evolutionary Fitness scale: A measure of the independent criterion of fitness. *EvoS Journal: The Journal of the Evolutionary Studies Consortium, 7*(1), 181–205.

Hamilton, W. D. (1964). The genetical evolution of social behavior. I and II. *Journal of Theoretical Biology, 7*, 1–52.

Lennox, J. G. (1991). Commentary on Byerly and Michod. *Biology and Philosophy, 6*, 33–37.

MacArthur, R. H., & Wilson, E. O. (1967). *The theory of island biogeography*. Princeton, NJ: Princeton University Press.

Michod, R. E. (1999). *Darwinian dynamics: Evolutionary transitions in fitness and individuality*. Princeton, NJ: Princeton University Press.

Pianka, E. R. (1970). On r- and K-selection. *American Naturalist, 104*, 592–596.

Pianka, E. R. (1978). *Evolutionary psychology*. New York, NY: Harper & Row.

Rosenberg, A. (1983). Fitness. *The Journal of Philosophy, 80*(8), 457. https://doi.org/10.2307/2026163

Rowe, D. C., Vazsonyi, A. T., & Figueredo, A. J. (1997). Mating effort in adolescence: Conditional or alternative strategy? *Journal of Personality and Individual Differences, 23*, 105–115.

Rushton, J. P. (1985). Differential K theory: The sociobiology of individual and group differences. *Personality and Individual Differences, 6*, 441–452.

Sober, E. (1993). *Philosophy of biology*. Boulder, CO: Westview Press.

Trivers, R. L. (1971). The evolution of reciprocal altruism. *The Quarterly Review of Biology, 46*(1), 35–57. https://doi.org/10.1086/406755

Wenner, C. J., Figueredo, A. J., & Jacobs, W. J. (2005). *Validation of the "Mini-K" using socially problematic behaviors*. Annual Meeting of the Human Behavior and Evolution Society. Presented at the Austin, TX

Woodley, M., de Baca, T. C., Fernandes, H. B. F., Madison, G., Figueredo, A.-J., & Aguirre, M. P. (2017). Slow and steady wins the race: K positively predicts fertility in the USA and Sweden. *Evolutionary Psychological Science, 3*(2), 109–117. https://doi.org/10.1007/s40806-016-0077-1

Chapter 3
Evolutionary Psychopathology and Depression

3.1 Brief Introduction

Evolutionary psychopathology is the evolutionary discipline that attempts to understand and explain the causes of mental disorders from an evolutionary perspective. Evolutionary psychology and evolutionary psychopathology start from the foundation of a universal human nature (Buss, 2000; Tooby & Cosmides, 1990) and converge on two principles: (1) that there is a *universal human nature* that has evolved through natural selection, and (2) that some modern environments are toxic and damaging, given our evolved nature. For instance, just as junk food damages our physical health, so do deviations from ancestral patterns of kinship and group cohesion (e.g., band and tribal patterns) damage our mental health (Gilbert & Bailey, 2000).

The high and persistent incidence of mental disorder in the general population has triggered attempts to explain it from an evolutionary perspective. Such attempts generally center on a taxonomy or definition of mental disorder (Wakefield, 1997; Wakefield & First, 2003) or on the possible functions of distinct mental conditions (Crow, 1991, 1995, 1997; Fiske & Haslam, 1997; Mealey, 2000). To this end, a mental disorder is seen either as evolutionary dysfunction/failure of natural design (e.g., phobias), or as naturally selected conditions (e.g., mild depression) having present or past fitness advantages (Nesse, 2005)).

Evolutionary psychopathology offers explanations for many mental symptoms and conditions. For instance, phobias, in this view, are the result of evolved mechanisms designed to yield false positives, rather than false negatives. Indeed, just one false negative (e.g., *not* avoiding a poisonous snake, believing it is harmless) could have resulted in death in ancestral environments (Nesse, 2005). Evolutionary psychologists argue that many phobias are exaggerations of fears of situations and objects that constituted threats in our evolutionary past (e.g., spiders, heights, storms, snakes, blood). Indeed, studies show that few people develop phobias of

C. Giosan, *Cognitive Evolutionary Therapy for Depression*, SpringerBriefs in Psychology, https://doi.org/10.1007/978-3-030-38874-4_3

modern threats to survival, such as pollution or cigarettes (Marks, 1987; Marks & Nesse, 1994).

3.2 Depression and Fitness

When a behavior (or symptom) has universality, a legitimate question about its possible biological/evolutionary function arises and, in many cases, the answers center on the potential fitness advantages of that behavior.

Depression, because of its high prevalence (5–10% in the US, (Kessler et al., 2003), cross-cultural universality (Nesse & Williams, 1996) upward course in symptom severity (NIMS, 1994), and puzzling potential fitness consequences, including suicide (APA, 1994; Fisher & Thomson, 2007), has received special attention in the evolutionary psychology literature.

Although no single cause for depression has been unequivocally identified, factors such as demographics and prior major depression (Lewinsohn, Hoberman, & Rosenbaum, 1988), early traumatic experiences (e.g., physical or sexual abuse) (Heim, Owens, Plotsky, & Nemeroff, 1997; Maercker, Michael, Fehm, Becker, & Margraf, 2004), or negative life experiences (e.g., job loss, loss of a close one) (Shrout et al., 1989), are believed to be involved.

While low mood is seen by evolutionary psychologists as *functional*, major depression is viewed as an example of modern pathology, whereby an adaptive response has gone awry. This view is supported by the evidence that depression is more prevalent in modern, Western cultures with loosely structured and dense populations that have little resemblance to the ancestral communities (Gilbert, 1992; McGuire, Troisi, & Raleigh, 1997) and by the observation that it can have serious negative consequences to fitness, such as suicide (Fisher & Thomson, 2007; McGuire et al., 1997).

In stark contrast to the prevalent view that depression is a brain disorder (Andreasen, 1985; Valenstein, 1998; Wolpert, 1999), evolutionary psychologists attempt to explain it in reference to the functions it may serve. For instance, Leith and Baumeister (1996) showed that low mood is associated with lesser likelihood of engaging in risk taking behaviors, and other researchers have argued that low levels of depression appear to be 'normal' or functional states (Hagen, 2003; McGuire et al., 1997; Nesse, 1998).

Some scholars view depression as a mechanism that blocks unfavorable investments, which will motivate changes in behavioral strategies and goal pursuit (Watson & Andrews, 2002). In the same view, researchers have reported positive associations between depression and occupational functioning, associations that might develop as a result of depression-related reassessment and attempts to change the strategy (Buist-Bouwman, Ormel, de Graaf, & Vollebergh, 2004; Williams, 1966).

Other studies have uncovered links between certain types of fitness strategies (e.g., Life History) and depression. For instance, Giosan (2013) showed that a high-K strategy is an important negative predictor of depressive symptomatology, accounting for 15% of the variance in Beck Depression Inventory scores (Beck, Steer, & Brown, 1996) after controlling for risk factors for depression.

Others scholars view depression as a result of unsuccessful attempts to reach a critical goal, and clinicians note that depression sometimes subsides when the individual gives up the pursuit of an unattainable goal (Nesse, 2000; Price, Sloman, Gardner, Gilbert, & Rohde, 1994; Wrosch, Scheier, & Carver, 2003). A specific type of depression – postpartum – is seen by other evolutionary scholars as a mechanism that signals fitness costs, which motivates the mother to reduce the investment in her child (Hagen, 2002). This view is supported by the evidence that the correlates of postpartum depression include lack of social support, especially from the father (Campbell, Cohn, Flanagan, Popper, & Meyers, 1992; Paykel, Emms, Fletcher, & Rassaby, 1980; Richman, Raskin, & Gaines, 1991) and/or infant problems (Atkinson & Rickel, 1984; Campbell & Cohn, 1991; Campbell et al., 1992; Kumar & Robson, 1984).

Yet other scholars view depression as an adaptation that serves the purpose of inhibiting aggressive behaviors toward others of superior rank (Evans, 1999; Price et al., 1994). This view of "involuntary yielding" draws on observations of individuals from various animal species that have lost their status in the hierarchy (Gilbert, 1992; Sloman, Price, Gilbert, & Gardner, 1994).

Although different, many of the above-mentioned evolutionary explanations of depression consider it a mechanism that can contribute to fitness (for a synthesis of the major adaptationist perspectives of depression, see Durisko, Mulsant, & Andrews, 2015). Evolutionary psychologists note that when humans are successful at meeting fitness-enhancing goals, they generally experience well-being and happiness (Gilbert & Bailey, 2000). On the other hand, failure (perceived or real) to meet these challenges results in dissatisfaction, depression, tension, or frustration (Gilbert & Bailey, 2000).

3.3 Depression and the Mismatch Hypothesis

Different groups are affected differentially by depression. The Amish, for instance, are the only one known group of Americans not affected by depression (Ilardi, 2009). Similarly, hunter-gatherer tribes, such as the Kaluli people, have virtually no rates of clinical depression (Ilardi, 2009). In contrast, developed countries, such as the UK, Germany or US, have witnessed alarming increases in depression rates. In the United States, depression rates have historically increased despite a parallel increase in antidepressant use. In line with this trend, in third-world countries the prevalence of depression, once very low, has increased as people have shifted from traditional to modern lifestyles (Ilardi, 2009).

These findings cannot be explained by cross-cultural or historical confounds, as they have also been yielded by cross-sectional studies within the same cultures as well, which documented significant differences in the prevalence of depression (and anxiety disorders) between rural and urban populations (Kennedy & Adolphs, 2011).

The observation that depression is more prevalent in the modern societies has led some authors to make the argument that this condition is the result of a misfit or a mismatch between our evolved adaptations and the present environments (Nesse & Williams, 1996). This argument stems from the broader "Mismatch Hypothesis", which is a theory in evolutionary biology describing how some traits that conferred benefits in the past are now maladaptive because of environmental changes (Lloyd, Wilson, & Sober, 2011). Example of outcomes of such mismatches include obesity and diabetes (Knight, 2011) (see also Appendix 1), osteoporosis (Lieberman, 2013), the effects of hygiene on inflammation (Garn & Renz, 2007), gambling (Spinella, 2003), drug use (Durrant, Adamson, Todd, & Sellman, 2009), or compulsive overeating (Davis & Carter, 2009).

From this perspective, depression is seen as the result of a mismatch between our evolved adaptations and the environments we currently live in. This made some authors address depression in therapy by outlining some practical steps to reduce such misfits. For instance, the *Therapeutic Lifestyle Change for Depression* protocol (Karwoski, Prohaska, Stites, Steidtmann, & Ilardi, 2005), incorporates several evolutionary elements that are thought to have positive effects on mood. They are (1) Omega-3 fatty acid consumption, (2) Bright light exposure, (3) Sleep hygiene, (4) Aerobic exercises, (5) Anti-rumination exercises, and (6) Social support.

References

Andreasen, N. C. (1985). *The broken brain: The biological revolution in psychiatry*. New York, NY: William Morrow Paperbacks.

APA. (1994). *Diagnostic and statistical manual of mental disorders* (4th ed.). Washington, DC: APA.

Atkinson, A. K., & Rickel, A. U. (1984). Postpartum depression in primiparous parents. *Journal of Abnormal Psychology, 93*(1), 115–119.

Beck, A. T., Steer, A. R., & Brown, G. K. (1996). *Manual for the beck depression inventory—II*. San Antonio, TX: The Psychological Corporation.

Buist-Bouwman, M. A., Ormel, J., de Graaf, R., & Vollebergh, W. A. M. (2004). Functioning after a major depressive episode: Complete or incomplete recovery? *Journal of Affective Disorders, 82*(3), 363–371. https://doi.org/10.1016/j.jad.2004.02.007

Buss, D. M. (2000). *The dangerous passion: Why jealousy is as necessary as love and sex*. New York, NY: Free Press.

Campbell, S. B., & Cohn, J. F. (1991). Prevalence and correlates of postpartum depression in first-time mothers. *Journal of Abnormal Psychology, 100*(4), 594–599.

Campbell, S. B., Cohn, J. F., Flanagan, C., Popper, S., & Meyers, T. (1992). Course and correlates of postpartum depression during the transition to parenthood. *Development and Psychopathology, 4*(01), 29–47. https://doi.org/10.1017/S095457940000554X

Crow, T. J. (1991). Origins of psychosis and the "Descent of Man". *British Journal of Psychiatry, 159*, 76–82.

Crow, T. J. (1995). A Darwinian approach to the origins of psychosis. *British Journal of Psychiatry, 167*, 12–25.

Crow, T. J. (1997). Is schizophrenia the price that Homo Sapiens pays for language? *Schizophrenia Research, 28*, 127–141.

Davis, C., & Carter, J. C. (2009). Compulsive overeating as an addiction disorder. A review of theory and evidence. *Appetite, 53*(1), 1–8. https://doi.org/10.1016/j.appet.2009.05.018

Durisko, Z., Mulsant, B. H., & Andrews, P. W. (2015). An adaptationist perspective on the etiology of depression. *Journal of Affective Disorders, 172*, 315–323. https://doi.org/10.1016/j.jad.2014.09.032

Durrant, R., Adamson, S., Todd, F., & Sellman, D. (2009). Drug use and addiction: Evolutionary perspective. *Australian and New Zealand Journal of Psychiatry, 43*(11), 1049–1056. https://doi.org/10.3109/00048670903270449

Evans, D. (1999). The social competition hypothesis of depression. *The ASCAP Newsletter, 12*, 12–15.

Fisher, H. E., & Thomson, J. A. J. (2007). Lust, romance, attachment: Do the side effects of serotonin-enhancing antidepressants jeopardize romantic love, marriage and fertility? In S. M. Platek, J. P. Keenan, & T. K. Shackelford (Eds.), *Evolutionary cognitive neuroscience*. Cambridge, MA: MIT Press.

Fiske, A. P., & Haslam, N. (1997). Is obsessive-compulsive disorder a pathology of the human disposition to perform socially meaningful rituals? Evidence of similar content. *The Journal of Mental Disease, 185*, 211–222.

Garn, H., & Renz, H. (2007). Epidemiological and immunological evidence for the hygiene hypothesis. *Immunobiology, 212*(6), 441–452. https://doi.org/10.1016/j.imbio.2007.03.006

Gilbert, P. (1992). *Depression: The evolution of powerlessness* (2nd ed.). Hove, UK: Psychology Press.

Gilbert, P., & Bailey, K. G. (Eds.). (2000). *Genes on the couch: Explorations in evolutionary psychotherapy*. Hove, UK: Brunner-Routledge.

Giosan, C. (2013). 'Slow' reproductive strategy: A negative predictor of depressive symptomatology. *Australian Journal of Psychology, 65*(3), 156–162. https://doi.org/10.1111/ajpy.12016

Hagen, E. H. (2002). Depression as bargaining: The case postpartum. *Evolution and Human Behavior, 23*, 323–336.

Hagen, E. H. (2003). The bargaining model of depression. In P. Hammerstein (Ed.), *Genetic and cultural evolution of cooperation* (pp. 95–123). Cambridge, MA: MIT Press.

Heim, C., Owens, M. J., Plotsky, P. M., & Nemeroff, C. B. (1997). The role of early adverse life events in the etiology of depression and posttraumatic stress disorder. Focus on corticotropin-releasing factor. *Annals of the New York Academy of Science, 821*, 194–207.

Ilardi, S. S. (2009). *The depression cure: The 6-step program to beat depression without drugs*. Cambridge, MA: Da Capo Press.

Karwoski, L., Prohaska, J. A., Stites, B. A., Steidtmann, D., & Ilardi, S. S. (2005). *Therapeutic Lifestyle Change (TLC) for Depression: Initial results with a severely depressed outpatient population*. Poster presented at the American Psychological Association.

Kennedy, D. P., & Adolphs, R. (2011). Social neuroscience: Stress and the city. *Nature, 474*(7352), 452–453. https://doi.org/10.1038/474452a

Kessler, R. C., Berglund, P. A., Demler, O., Jin, R., Koretz, D., Merikangas, K. R., … Wang, P. S. (2003). The epidemiology of major depressive disorder: Results from the National Comorbidity Survey replication (NCS-R). *Journal of the American Medical Association, 289*, 3095–3105.

Knight, C. (2011). "Most people are simply not designed to eat pasta": Evolutionary explanations for obesity in the low-carbohydrate diet movement. *Public Understanding of Science, 20*(5), 706–719. https://doi.org/10.1177/0963662510391733

Kumar, R., & Robson, K. M. (1984). A prospective study of emotional disorders in childbearing women. *British Journal of Psychiatry, 144*, 35–47.

Leith, K. P., & Baumeister, R. (1996). Why do moods increase self-defeating behavior? Emotion, risk-taking and self-regulation. *Journal of Personality and Social Psychology, 71*, 1250–1267.

Lewinsohn, P. M., Hoberman, H. M., & Rosenbaum, M. (1988). A prospective study of risk factors for unipolar depression. *Journal of Abnormal Psychology, 97*, 251–264.

Lieberman, D. E. (2013). *The story of the human body: Evolution, health, and disease*. New York, NY: Pantheon Books.

Lloyd, E., Wilson, D. S., & Sober, E. (2011). Evolutionary mismatch and what to do about it: A basic tutorial. *Evolutionary Applications*, 2–4.

Maercker, A., Michael, T., Fehm, L., Becker, E. S., & Margraf, J. (2004). Age of traumatisation as a predictor of posttraumatic stress disorder or major depression in young women. *British Journal of Psychiatry, 184*, 482–487.

Marks, I. M. (1987). *Fears, phobias, and rituals*. New York, NY: Oxford University Press.

Marks, I. M., & Nesse, R. M. (1994). Fear and fitness: An evolutionary analysis of anxiety disorders. *Ethology and Sociobiology, 15*, 247–261.

McGuire, M. T., Troisi, A., & Raleigh, M. M. (1997). Depression in evolutionary context. In S. Baron-Cohen (Ed.), *The maladapted mind: Classic readings in evolutionary psychopathology*. London, UK: Erlbaum/Taylor & Francis.

Mealey, L. (2000). Anorexia: A "losing" strategy? *Human Nature, 11*, 105–116.

Nesse, R. M. (1998). Emotional disorders in evolutionary perspective. *British Journal of Medical Psychology, 71*, 397–415.

Nesse, R. M. (2000). Is depression an adaptation? *Archives of General Psychiatry, 57*, 14–20.

Nesse, R. M. (2005). Natural selection and the regulation of defenses: A signal detection analysis of the smoke detector principle. *Evolution and Human Behavior, 26*, 88–105.

Nesse, R. M., & Williams, G. C. (1996). *Why we get sick: The new science of Darwinian medicine* (1st ed.). New York, NY: Vintage.

NIMS. (1994). *Depression fact sheet*. Bethesda, MD: National Institutes of Health.

Paykel, E. S., Emms, E. M., Fletcher, J., & Rassaby, E. S. (1980). Life events and social support in puerperal depression. *British Journal of Psychiatry, 136*, 229–346.

Price, J. S., Sloman, L., Gardner, R., Gilbert, P., & Rohde, P. (1994). The social competition hypothesis of depression. *British Journal of Psychiatry, 64*, 309–315.

Richman, J. A., Raskin, V. D., & Gaines, C. (1991). Gender roles, social support, and postpartum depressive symptomatology: The benefits of caring. *Journal of Nervous and Mental Disease, 179*, 139–147.

Shrout, P. E., Link, B. G., Dohrenwend, B. P., Skodol, A. E., Stueve, A., & Mirotznik, J. (1989). Characterizing life events as risk factors for depression: The role of fateful loss events. *Journal of Abnormal Psychology, 98*, 460–467.

Sloman, L., Price, J. S., Gilbert, P., & Gardner, R. (1994). Adaptive function of depression: Psychotherapeutic implications. *American Journal of Psychotherapy, 48*, 1–16.

Spinella, M. (2003). Evolutionary mismatch, neural reward circuits, and pathological gambling. *International Journal of Neuroscience, 113*(4), 503–512. https://doi.org/10.1080/00207450390162254

Tooby, J., & Cosmides, L. (1990). The past explains the present: Emotional adaptations and the structure of ancestral environments. *Ethology and Sociobiology, 11*, 375–424.

Valenstein, E. S. (1998). *Blaming the brain: The truth about drugs and mental health*. New York, NY: Free Press.

Wakefield, J. C. (1997). Diagnosing DSM-IV-Part 1: DSM-IV and the concept of disorder. *Behavior Research and Therapy, 35*, 633–649.

Wakefield, J. C., & First, M. (2003). Clarifying the distinction between disorder and non-disorder: Confronting the overdiagnosis ("false positives") problem in DSM-IV. In K. A. Phillips, M. B. First, & H. A. Pincus (Eds.), *Advancing DSM: Dilemmas in psychiatric diagnosis*. Washington, DC: American Psychiatric Press.

Watson, P. J., & Andrews, P. W. (2002). Toward a revised evolutionary adaptationist analysis of depression: The social navigation hypothesis. *Journal of Affective Disorders, 72*, 1–14.

Williams, G. C. (1966). *Adaptation and natural selection*. Princeton, NJ: Princeton University Press.

Wolpert, L. (1999). *Malignant sadness: The anatomy of depression*. New York, NY: Free Press.

Wrosch, C., Scheier, M. F., & Carver, C. S. (2003). The importance of goal disengagement in adaptive self-regulation: When giving up is beneficial. *Self and Identity, 2*, 1–20.

Chapter 4
The Current Psychological Standard of Care in Depression

Currently, there are many treatment approaches to depression, among which the most widely used are: (1) Cognitive Behavioral therapy, (2) Mindfulness-based Cognitive Therapy, (3) Behavioral Activation, and (4) Interpersonal Psychotherapy.

4.1 Cognitive-Behavioral Therapy

Cognitive-Behavioral Therapy (CBT) is an umbrella term used to describe both standard Cognitive Therapy (CT) and the atheoretical combination of CT and behavioral strategies (A. T. Beck, 2005). Cognitive Therapy, the prototype of CBT, was developed for the treatment of depression (A. T. Beck, 1976, 1979). It is a structured, goals-oriented, short-term intervention organized around the concepts of automatic thoughts and schema/core beliefs (J. S. Beck, 1995; David & Szentagotai, 2006). Cognitive Therapy focuses on specific current problems, using techniques designed to modify dysfunctional thinking and targeting problematic behaviors (J. S. Beck, 1995).

Regardless of the specific approach, all CBT-based treatments generally have some common features. First, most involve two fundamental intervention areas: (1) *cognitive restructuring*, designed to change faulty thinking patterns, and (2) *behavioral techniques*, designed to increase or decrease the occurrence, frequency or intensity of target behaviors. Second, all the CBT-based therapies focus on the immediate present and on specific problems. Moreover, they all are goal-oriented (goals are defined collaboratively for every session) and time-limited. Finally, the approach is educational (i.e., patients are provided structured learning experiences and are taught coping skills) and patients have an active role in the therapeutic process, during the sessions and between sessions. The patients are given homework assignments for every session and are encouraged to identify specific ways to practice newly acquired skills.

C. Giosan, *Cognitive Evolutionary Therapy for Depression*, SpringerBriefs in Psychology, https://doi.org/10.1007/978-3-030-38874-4_4

CBT is one of the treatments of choice for depression, recommended by leading mental health agencies such as the National Institute for Clinical Excellence (www.nice.org.uk) or the National Institute for Mental Health (www.nimh.nih.gov). Numerous studies attest the efficacy of this well-established approach in the treatment of depression (Watts, Turnell, Kladnitski, Newby, & Andrews, 2015).

4.2 Mindfulness-Based Cognitive Therapy

Mindfulness-based Cognitive Therapy (MBCT), an eight-week manualized group intervention, was originally developed to prevent relapse among those in remission from depression and/or for those who suffer from chronic depression (Segal, Williams, & Teasdale, 2002). It recognizes the role of negative mental processes (e.g., cognitive biases such as the preferential processing of negative information) and contents (e.g., negative automatic thoughts) in the onset and maintenance of depression, as well as the fact that these internal experiences are rather mental events than actual realities. Unlike CBT, this approach does not employ an effort to change dysfunctional cognitions but teaches patients to be mindful and non-judgmental about their internal experiences. The goal of this approach is to help patients to distance emotionally from automatic and self-perpetuating cognitions characteristic of depression.

MBCT was found to be as effective as CBT in the treatment of depression (Manicavasgar, Parker, & Perich, 2011), and significantly better than standard of care alone in preventing relapses in patients with three or more prior depressive episodes (Chiesa & Serretti, 2011; Keng, Smoski, & Robins, 2011).

4.3 Behavioral Activation

Behavioral activation builds on Lewinsohn's (1974) emphasis of the role of response-contingent positive reinforcements as proximal causes of depressive symptoms. In this view, depression results from desirable behaviors reinforced increasingly less, due to losses or reduction of response-contingent reinforcers. At the same time, counterproductive behaviors, such as social isolation or excessive sadness, may be unintentionally reinforced by the (social) environment, resulting in the maintenance of the depressive symptoms.

Two treatment approaches based on behavioral strategies are: (1) *Behavioral Activation* (Martell, Addis, & Jacobson, 2001) and (2) *Behavioral Activation Treatment for Depression* (Lejuez, Hopko, LePage, Hopko, & McNeil, 2001).

1. *Behavioral Activation* includes techniques commonly used in cognitive therapy, such as activity scheduling, daily activity monitoring, stimulus control procedures, skills training (when needed), mental rehearsal of assigned behavior, and

contingency management, whose purpose is to facilitate access to reinforcements. Behavioral Activation does not focus on pleasurable activities, but rather on the functional analysis of behavior and the client's goal, embracing an idiographic functional approach (Manos, Kanter, & Busch, 2010). Customized interventions are designed and implemented by the careful examination of antecedents and consequences of target behaviors. Behavioral Activation also highlights the role of aversive stimuli (punishers and negative reinforcers) in relation to depression and targets avoidance patterns in treatment, replacing them with more adaptive coping behaviors.

2. *Behavioral Activation Treatment for Depression* expands Lewinsohn's (1974) original approach by emphasizing positive and negative reinforcements in relation to both depressive and non-depressive behaviors and by taking into account the client's values (Lejuez et al., 2001). It aims to differentially reinforce depressive and non-depressive behaviors, increasing the value and availability of reinforcers for non-depressed behaviors while decreasing the value and availability of reinforcers for depressive behavior. Another distinctive note of this intervention is the direct targeting of the person's environment, by involving family and friends who sign behavioral contracts designed to decrease the patient's access to positive reinforcement (i.e., attention) and negative reinforcement (i.e., avoidance of unpleasant tasks) for depressed behaviors, and increase reinforcement for non-depressed behaviors (Manos et al., 2010).

Systematic reviews and meta-analyses (Dimidjian, Barrera, Martell, Muñoz, & Lewinsohn, 2011; Mazzucchelli, Kane, & Rees, 2009) show that Behavioral Activation is well-established, empirically-validated treatment for depression.

4.4 Interpersonal Psychotherapy (IPT)

Interpersonal psychotherapy (IPT) for depression focuses on improving interpersonal difficulties and emphasizes the role of *social support* to the onset and maintenance of depression. Interpersonal difficulties are thought to trigger or exacerbate depressive symptoms. In fact, depression and interpersonal difficulties are assumed to reciprocally influence each another. Thus, the rationale behind IPT is that improvement in interpersonal relationships leads to improvement in depressive symptoms, which loops back to cause better interpersonal functioning (Kelly, Cyranowski, & Frank, 2007).

IPT has been shown to be an efficacious treatment for depression in numerous clinical trials (Cuijpers, 2011; Jakobsen, 2011; Mufson, 2008; Mufson et al., 2004; Mufson, Weissman, Moreau, & Garfinkel, 1999) and it one of the recommended treatments of choice by the National Institute for Clinical Excellence (NICE; see www.nice.org.uk) and the National Institute of Mental Health (https://www.nimh.nih.gov).

References

Beck, A. T. (1976). *Cognitive therapy and the emotional disorders*. New York, NY: International Universities Press.

Beck, A. T. (1979). *Cognitive therapy of depression*. New York, NY: Guilford Press.

Beck, A. T. (2005). The current state of cognitive therapy: A 40-year retrospective. *Archives of General Psychiatry, 62*(9), 953–959. https://doi.org/10.1001/archpsyc.62.9.953

Beck, J. S. (1995). *Cognitive therapy: Basics and beyond* (1st ed.). New York, NY: The Guilford Press.

Chiesa, A., & Serretti, A. (2011). Mindfulness based cognitive therapy for psychiatric disorders: A systematic review and meta-analysis. *Psychiatry Research, 187*(3), 441–453. https://doi.org/10.1016/j.psychres.2010.08.011

Cuijpers, P. (2011). The patient perspective in research on major depression. *BMC Psychiatry, 11*, 89. https://doi.org/10.1186/1471-244X-11-89

David, D., & Szentagotai, A. (2006). Cognitions in cognitive-behavioral psychotherapies; toward an integrative model. *Clinical Psychology Review, 26*(3), 284–298. https://doi.org/Review

Dimidjian, S., Barrera, M., Martell, C., Muñoz, R. F., & Lewinsohn, P. M. (2011). The origins and current status of behavioral activation treatments for depression. *Annual Review of Clinical Psychology, 7*(1), 1–38. https://doi.org/10.1146/annurev-clinpsy-032210-104535

Jakobsen, J. C. (2011). Review: Interpersonal psychotherapy is effective as an acute or maintenance treatment for unipolar depression. *Evidence-Based Mental Health, 14*(4), 108. https://doi.org/Comment

Kelly, M. A., Cyranowski, J. M., & Frank, E. (2007). Sudden gains in interpersonal psychotherapy for depression. *Behaviour Research and Therapy, 45*(11), 2563–2572. https://doi.org/Research Support, N.I.H., Extramural.

Keng, S. L., Smoski, M. J., & Robins, C. J. (2011). Effects of mindfulness on psychological health: A review of empirical studies. *Clinical Psychology Review, 31*(6), 1041–1056. https://doi.org/10.1016/j.cpr.2011.04.006

Lejuez, C. W., Hopko, D. R., LePage, J. P., Hopko, S. D., & McNeil, D. W. (2001). A brief behavioral activation treatment for depression. *Cognitive and Behavioral Practice, 8*(2), 164–175. https://doi.org/10.1016/S1077-7229(01)80022-5

Lewinsohn, P. M. (1974). Clinical and theorethical aspects of depression. In *Innovative treatment methods in psychopathology*. New York, NY: Wiley.

Manicavasgar, V., Parker, G., & Perich, T. (2011). Mindfulness-based cognitive therapy vs cognitive behaviour therapy as a treatment for non-melancholic depression. *Journal of Affective Disorders, 130*, 138–144.

Manos, R. C., Kanter, J. W., & Busch, A. M. (2010). A critical review of assessment strategies to measure the behavioral activation model of depression. *Clinical Psychology Review, 30*(5), 547–561. https://doi.org/Review

Martell, C. R., Addis, M. E., & Jacobson, N. S. (2001). *Depression in context: Strategies for guided action*. Retrieved from http://books.google.ro/books?id=Zcq7QgAACAAJ

Mazzucchelli, T., Kane, R., & Rees, C. (2009). Behavioral activation treatments for depression in adults: A meta-analysis and review. *Clinical Psychology: Science and Practice, 16*(4), 383–411.

Mufson, L. (2008). Group interpersonal therapy reduces depression in adolescent survivors of war. *Evidence-Based Mental Health, 11*(1), 17. https://doi.org/Comment

Mufson, L., Dorta, K. P., Wickramaratne, P., Nomura, Y., Olfson, M., & Weissman, M. M. (2004). A randomized effectiveness trial of interpersonal psychotherapy for depressed adolescents. *Archives of General Psychiatry, 61*(6), 577–584. https://doi.org/Clinical Trial Comparative Study Randomized Controlled Trial Research Support, U.S. Gov't, P.H.S.

Mufson, L., Weissman, M. M., Moreau, D., & Garfinkel, R. (1999). Efficacy of interpersonal psychotherapy for depressed adolescents. *Archives of General Psychiatry, 56*(6), 573–579. https://

doi.org/Clinical Trial Comparative Study Randomized Controlled Trial Research Support, U.S. Gov't, P.H.S.

Segal, Z. V., Williams, J. M. G., & Teasdale, J. D. (2002). *Mindfulness-based cognitive therapy for depression: A new approach to preventing relapse*. Retrieved from http://books.google.ro/books?id=_QJ3cQT5UPsC

Watts, S. E., Turnell, A., Kladnitski, N., Newby, J. M., & Andrews, G. (2015). Treatment-as-usual (TAU) is anything but usual: A meta-analysis of CBT versus TAU for anxiety and depression. *Journal of Affective Disorders, 175*, 152–167. https://doi.org/10.1016/j.jad.2014.12.025

Chapter 5
Cognitive Evolutionary Therapy for Depression

A Rwandan man once described the Rwandan treatment for depression to the 2001 National Book Award winner Andrew Solomon in these words: "*You know, we had a lot of trouble with Western mental health workers, especially the ones who came here right after the genocide. They came and their practice did not involve being outside in the sunshine... which is, after all, where you begin to feel better. There was no drumming or music to get your blood flowing again – when you're depressed and low you need to have your blood flowing. There was no sense that everyone had taken the day off so that the entire community could come together to lift you up and bring you back to joy. There was no acknowledgement of the depression as something invasive and external that could actually be cast out of you again. Instead, they would take people one at a time into these dingy little rooms and have them sit around for an hour or so to talk about bad things that had happened to them. We had to ask them to leave the country.*" (Taljaard, n.d.)

While this description of a psychological intervention for depression is in stark contrast with the standard weekly therapy sessions so common in the Western cultures, it would not make an evolutionary therapist surprised. As we will see in the sections that follow, Cognitive Evolutionary Therapy (CET) for depression does borrow insights from such approaches.

5.1 Conceptualization in Psychotherapy

Clinical conceptualization is an explanation of problems and their causes provided by the therapist to the patient. To be efficient, this explanation should provide an accurate description of the: (1) mental problem; (2) probable causes of the mental problem; (3) ethiopathogenetic processes involved; (4) positive/adverse effects of the treatment. When the therapist successfully addresses these areas, she creates

C. Giosan, *Cognitive Evolutionary Therapy for Depression*, SpringerBriefs in Psychology, https://doi.org/10.1007/978-3-030-38874-4_5

sense of prediction and control in the patient, raising the hope of getting better and leading to positive expectancies of the treatment's outcome (John & Segal, 2014; Kuyken, Padesky, & Dudley, 2008a, 2008b).

The first record of clinical conceptualization was Freud's interpretation of neurotic symptoms and latent content of the dreams. This interpretation, Freud argued, could unravel parts of the unconsciousness, thus leading to catharsis and healing (Freud & Brill, 1915).

Miller, Duncan, and Hubble (1997) argued that there are four common factors to all psychotherapies that determine their success: client factors, therapist factors, placebo and specific techniques. Asay and Lambert (1999) evaluated these factors and showed that the therapeutic success is 40% due to client factors, 30% to therapist factors, 15% due to placebo, expectancy and hope, and 15% due to specific psychotherapeutic techniques. The third factor (placebo, expectancy and hope) refers to the client' and therapist's belief in the rationale and efficiency of the treatment – i.e., conceptualization. A good understanding of the problem and the link between the problem and the treatment suggested by the therapist can make the treatment more credible and the patient more involved, leading to better treatment outcomes, such as reduced dropout rate and increased treatment adherence.

5.2 Cognitive Evolutionary Therapy for Depression and Clinical Conceptualization

5.2.1 The ABC/ABCDE Model

Some authors have suggested that an integrative understanding of behavior must include a *proximate* and an *ultimate (functional)* analysis of behavior, as well as an understanding of both phylogenetic/developmental history and the operation of current mechanisms (Tinbergen, 1963). For instance, some scholars argue that Beck's cognitive distortions (Beck, 1979) are a *consequence* of depression, not a *cause* of it (Dobson & Shaw, 1987), pointing to the necessity of additional explicative layers.

The typical conceptualization in classical CBT only contains information about the first two questions (ontogeny and mechanisms of causation), that is, the proximal causes of psychopathology. In other words, the conceptualization in classical CBT answers the "how" questions, as illustrated by the ABC model (Ellis, 1994; Ellis, Dryden, & DiGiuseppe, 2007) presented in Fig. 5.1.

The original ABC theoretic conceptualization framework described above was later expanded into the ABCDE model (Ellis, 1994; Ellis et al. 2007) in recognition of the importance of disputation and replacing irrational beliefs with rational ones. In the ABCDE framework, (A) stands for undesirable life events ("activating events") that can be (1) internal or external, (2) past, present or future, or (3) real or imagined. People hold (B) rational or irrational beliefs about the activating events,

A	B	C
Activating life events (trigger-learned irrational beliefs)	Irrational Beliefs 1. Demandingness: "Things MUST be as I wish them to be." 2. Awfulizing: "I refuse to accept being shown up as foolish, as I must not be, and it is awful when I am." 3. Low Frustration Tolerance: "I refuse to accept that things in my life are hard and uncomfortable, as they must not be, and I can't stand it when they are." 4. Damnation / Global Evaluation: "I refuse to accept your treating me this way, as you must not, and you are no damned good for doing so."	Behavioral and emotional consequences (symptoms)

Fig. 5.1 The ABC model. (Ellis, 1994; Ellis et al., 2007)

which result in (C) affective, psycho-physiological and behavioral consequences. Rational beliefs (RBs) lead to functional consequences, while irrational beliefs (IBs) lead to dysfunctional consequences (Ellis et al., 2007). Once generated, the Cs can later convert to an A, triggering other rational/irrational beliefs (RBs/IBs), which will lead to other adaptive or maladaptive consequences. In order to change the dysfunctional consequences of their irrational thoughts, the patients are encouraged to actively (D) dispute these beliefs and replace them with more (E) efficient beliefs (Walen, DiGiuseppe, & Dryden, 1992).

5.2.2 *Cognitive Evolutionary Therapy as Clinical Conceptualization*

An evolutionary-enhanced psychotherapy for depression enhances the ABCDE model by including information about the hypothesized *adaptive* functions (the "why" questions) of depressive symptoms, along with direct interventions on fitness-enhancing factors. Thus, an evolutionary-inspired psychotherapy for depression enhances the conceptualization of the therapy and the therapy protocol by addressing the *distal* causes of depression (i.e., the evolutionary mechanisms involved) and explaining why depression is thought to be, in some cases, an expected response to a post-EEA environment (see Fig. 5.2).

Standard ABCDE model (CBT)	A Activating life events	B Beliefs	C Emotional and behavioral consequences	D Disputing (Cognitive restructuring)	E New, effective emotions and behaviors
Evolutionary Enhancements (CET)	Focus on fitness related activating events; select potential A's based on mismatch theory (using EFS)	Conceptualize irrational beliefs and dysfunctional emotions as adaptive mental structures left over from EEA		Normalize expectations (mismatch theory)	Prediction, control, self-acceptance

Fig. 5.2 The ABCDE model coupled with CET

5.3 Why Such an Intervention?

According to the World Health Organization, depression is the *leading* cause of disability worldwide ("WHO | "Depression," n.d.). Meta-analyses indicate that all bona fide (non-placebo) psychological treatments for depression (CBT included) are equally efficacious (Wampold, Minami, Baskin, & Tierney, 2002), with effect sizes ranging from small to moderate (Cuijpers, Smit, Bohlmeijer, Hollon, & Andersson, 2010). Given the exorbitant costs of this condition, the need to develop new approaches that add therapeutic value is vital. Even a 1% increase in treatment efficacy can translate into substantial cost savings.

Psychotherapists normally focus on events within the lifespan of a patient and examine proximal (mechanistic) causes of maladaptive behaviors, such as irrational or automatic thoughts (Beck, Rush, Shaw, & Emery, 1979). Modifying these thoughts has proven effective in ameliorating depressive symptoms. However, what is lacking in all the current psychological treatments for depression, including CBT, is a unifying paradigm providing explanations about the *ultimate* causes of depression. In other words, the underlying evolutionary factors that can lead to depression and biased thinking are not addressed directly in the current therapeutic approaches, unless specifically identified as problems by the patient, which only happen in a fraction of cases. Even in the cases when the patient does identify such factors, the therapy is empirically centered, lacking a unifying theory. Cognitive Evolutionary Therapy addresses both the proximate causes of depression (via cognitive therapy) and the distal causes (via evolutionary-based interventions).

5.4 Biosocial/Fitness Goals and Mental Health

Generally, in their evaluations, evolutionary psychotherapists turn their attention to unhealthy deviations from the human species norm and devise interventions aimed at normalizing such deviations (Gilbert & Bailey, 2000). Human behavior generally revolves around a finite set of fitness-relevant themes, such as shelter and security, status and resource acquisition, nutrition, sexual consummation within mateships, mating, parenting, or in-group and between-group interaction (Buss, 2005). Therefore, the main aim of an evolutionary therapist treating depression is to guide the patient towards solutions to the obstacles s/he is encountering in pursuing such biosocial goals. The role of the evolutionary therapist sometimes includes encouraging the patient to admit defeat in some of their pursuits for fitness-related goals and to seek fitness-related alternatives; compromising on morals when appropriate; recalibrating elevated expectations; making the patient give up unrealistic goal(s), since evolutionary research has shown that giving up pursuing unattainable goals can alleviate depression (Sloman, Price, Gilbert, & Gardner, 1994).

Some of these dimensions are sometimes also addressed in CBT, but *only in the cases where the patient specifically identifies problems related to them*. In many cases, however, people are not aware of the entire spectrum of (fitness) problems that might be linked to their depressive symptoms or might not even consider them important enough to bring to the clinician's attention. As described in detail in the next sections of this manual, CET's first step is to identify fitness-related problems at the beginning of the treatment and then devise appropriate interventions to address these problems.

The solutions advocated in evolutionary therapy can sometimes be extreme. The patient may be encouraged to buy a house or give one up (if it is judged that house ownership acts against the patient's fitness interests). The patient may be encouraged to begin preparations to move to a different area if there is a mismatch between her cultural background and the community in which she is residing. The patient may be encouraged to switch jobs or retrain for new jobs. The patient might even be encouraged, in some cases, to leave a partner, or find a new one (Keedwell, 2008).

Of course, the evolutionary therapist will never impose such solutions on to the patient. On the contrary, their implementation will only be attempted if they are generated by the patient, as a result of their understanding of the fitness-related factors that might contribute to their depression.

5.5 Efficacy of Cognitive Evolutionary Therapy for Depression

The efficacy of Cognitive Evolutionary Therapy for depression was examined in contrast to that of Cognitive Therapy in a Randomized Clinical Trial (Giosan, Cobeanu, et al., 2014) as well as in a case study (Giosan, Muresan, & Moldovan, 2014). The clinical trial included 97 depressive patients split in two active groups:

(1) the Cognitive Evolutionary Therapy (CET) group, who received cognitive evolutionary therapy and (2) the Cognitive Therapy (CT) group, who received standard cognitive therapy.

The results showed that the CET and CT protocols were equally efficacious, with the CET protocol showing a consistent pattern of larger gains during the treatment. CET was superior to CT at increasing engagement in social and enjoyable activities at posttreatment (d = 0.87, $p = .011$) and 3-month follow up (d = .28, $p = .524$) and showed greater reductions than the CT group in behavioral inhibition/avoidance at both post-treatment and follow-up (d = .72, $p = .016$) (Giosan et al., under review; Giosan et al., 2019).

References

Asay, T. P., & Lambert, M. J. (1999). The empirical case for the common factors in therapy: Quantitative findings. In *The heart and soul of change: What works in therapy* (pp. 23–55). Retrieved from http://psycnet.apa.org/books/11132/001

Beck, A. T. (1979). *Cognitive therapy of depression*. New York, NY: Guilford Press.

Beck, A. T., Rush, A. J., Shaw, B. F., & Emery, G. (1979). *Cognitive therapy of depression*. New York, NY: Guilford Press.

Buss, D. M. (2005). *The handbook of evolutionary psychology*. Hoboken, NJ: Wiley.

Cuijpers, P., Smit, F., Bohlmeijer, E., Hollon, S. D., & Andersson, G. (2010). Efficacy of cognitive–Behavioural therapy and other psychological treatments for adult depression: Meta-analytic study of publication bias. *The British Journal of Psychiatry, 196*, 173–178.

Dobson, K. S., & Shaw, B. F. (1987). Cognitive assessment with major depressive disorders. *Cognitive Therapy and Research, 10*(1), 13–29. https://doi.org/10.1007/BF01186286

Ellis, A. (1994). *Reason and emotion in psychotherapy*. Secaucus, NJ: Carol Pub. Group.

Ellis, A., Dryden, W., & DiGiuseppe, R. (2007). *The practice of rational emotive behavior therapy*. New York, NY: Springer.

Freud, S., & Brill, A. A. (1915). *The interpretation of dreams*. London, UK/New York, NY: G. Allen & Unwin, Limited.

Gilbert, P., & Bailey, K. G. (Eds.). (2000). *Genes on the couch: Explorations in evolutionary psychotherapy*. Hove, UK: Brunner-Routledge.

Giosan, C., Cobeanu, O., Wyka, K., Mureşan, V., Mogoaşe, C., Szentagotai, A., Malta, L.S., & Moldovan, R. (under review). Cognitive evolutionary therapy versus standard cognitive therapy for depression: A randomized clinical trial. Under review.

Giosan, C., Cobeanu, O., Mogoase, C., Muresan, V., Malta, L. S., Wyka, K., & Szentagotai, A. (2014). Evolutionary cognitive therapy versus standard cognitive therapy for depression: A protocol for a blinded, randomized, superiority clinical trial. *Trials, 15*(1), 83. https://doi.org/10.1186/1745-6215-15-83

Giosan, C., Cobeanu, O., Wyka, K., Muresan, V., Mogoase, C., Szentagotai, A., …, Moldovan, R. (2019, June 29). *Cognitive-evolutionary therapy for depression—Results of a randomized clinical trial*. Presented at the 31st Annual Human Behavior & Evolution Society Meeting, Boston, MA. Retrieved from http://meetatbu.com/hbes19/

Giosan, C., Muresan, V., & Moldovan, R. (2014). Cognitive evolutionary therapy for depression: A case study. *Clinical Case Reports, 2*(5), 228–236. https://doi.org/10.1002/ccr3.131

John, S., & Segal, D. L. (2014). Case conceptualization. In *The encyclopedia of clinical psychology*. https://doi.org/10.1002/9781118625392.wbecp106

Keedwell, P. (2008). *How sadness survived: The evolutionary basis of depression*. Oxford, UK: Radcliffe Publishing.

Kuyken, W., Padesky, C. A., & Dudley, R. (2008a). *Collaborative case conceptualization: Working effectively with clients in cognitive-behavioral therapy*. New York, NY: Guilford Press.

Kuyken, W., Padesky, C. A., & Dudley, R. (2008b). The science and practice of case conceptualization. *Behavioural and Cognitive Psychotherapy, 36*(6), 757–768. https://doi.org/10.1017/S1352465808004815

Miller, S. D., Duncan, B. L., & Hubble, M. A. (1997). *Escape from babel: Toward a unifying language for psychotherapy practice*. Retrieved from http://books.google.ro/books?id=OI19QgAACAAJ

Sloman, L., Price, J. S., Gilbert, P., & Gardner, R. (1994). Adaptive function of depression: Psychotherapeutic implications. *American Journal of Psychotherapy, 48*, 1–16.

Taljaard, T. (n.d.). *Treating depression with tribal wisdom*. Retrieved January 23, 2019, from https://upliftconnect.com/treating-depression-with-tribal-wisdom/

Tinbergen, N. (1963). On aims and methods of Ethology. *Zeitschrift für Tierpsychologie, 20*(4), 410–433. https://doi.org/10.1111/j.1439-0310.1963.tb01161.x

Walen, S. R., DiGiuseppe, R., & Dryden, W. (1992). *A practitioner's guide to rational-emotive therapy*. Retrieved from http://books.google.ro/books?id=wH-YiZnJgB8C

Wampold, B. E., Minami, T., Baskin, T. W., & Tierney, S. C. (2002). A meta-(re)analysis of the effects of cognitive therapy versus 'other therapies' for depression. *Journal of Affective Disorders, 68*, 159–165.

WHO | "Depression: Let's talk" says WHO, as depression tops list of causes of ill health. (n.d.). Retrieved February 18, 2018, from WHO website: http://www.who.int/mediacentre/news/releases/2017/world-health-day/en/

Chapter 6
Moral and Ethical Aspects in CET

6.1 Preliminary Considerations

Oftentimes, there is a divergence between behaviors that serve biosocial goals (i.e., behaviors that can enhance fitness) and the morality (or even the legality) of those behaviors.

Let's begin with two extreme examples: Male fitness can be achieved in multiple ways, one of which is rape, which some authors view as an evolved reproductive strategy (Thornhill & Palmer, 2000, 2004). In a similar vein, reproductive success can also be achieved by mating with underage opposite-sex partners. Both scenarios are examples of illegal acts in many societies, and widely (although not universally) regarded as immoral and repugnant.

Therefore, although evolutionary therapists must be mindful of the species' norms, they must also be mindful of legal and ethical concerns (both cultural and personal) and exclude any undesirable solutions. The above-mentioned examples are obvious and extreme, given to illustrate the point, but an evolutionary therapist might face situations in which the boundary between what is permissible and what is not is not so clear. For example, let us imagine that during therapy with a young, married male patient, one possible fitness-enhancing solution that the patient suggested (which would presumably decrease depression) was that the patient seek an extra-marital relationship. Let us also stretch our imagination and suppose that the moral aspects of this have been settled, in that the patient's wife has agreed to a one-way open marriage. In this scenario, should the therapist encourage the patient in this direction? The answer depends, among other concerns, on whether adulterous relationships (even with spousal consent) are legal in the respective society, and, if not, if the laws are enforced.

Furthermore, while evolutionary therapists must take into consideration the species norms, it must be added that these norms are high level and that there is considerable individual variation in pursuing biosocial goals. The evolutionary

C. Giosan, *Cognitive Evolutionary Therapy for Depression*, SpringerBriefs in Psychology, https://doi.org/10.1007/978-3-030-38874-4_6

therapist must incorporate this individual variation in the interventions. In other words, the aim of the therapist is to help the person become a biologically well-functioning member of the species, but not at the expense of that person's aspirations and needs. Ultimately, the role of the evolutionary therapist is to help the person to reasonably seek and meet biosocial goals, *as reflected in their personal aspirations and needs.*

The evolutionary therapist must also be cautious to label certain forms of thinking as pathological, because they may well be adaptive mechanisms at work (Gilbert & Bailey, 2000). Anxious thoughts, for instance ("distorted cognitions" in cognitive therapy), could be the activation of previously adaptive defensive information-processing whereby overestimating danger was more adaptive than underestimating it (Gilbert & Bailey, 2000). More often than not, biases and distortions, rather than logic, were the norm in our thinking and the role of these biases was to enhance fitness (Buss, 2000). Normalizing expectations can be therapeutic in such contexts.

Finally, the clients are not alone in therapy. Therapists themselves have biosocial goals, some of which are unconscious, which can interfere with the client's. Thus, the client-therapist relationship is considerably more nuanced as a result (Bailey, 2000; Kriegman, 2000). The therapists must be aware of their own biosocial goals and not allow them to interfere with the therapeutic process. For example, let's imagine that a male therapist finds a female patient very attractive. Let's further say that this patient is in a turbulent relationship with her partner. To serve his own biosocial goals, the therapist may (unintentionally or deliberately) guide her towards breaking up with her partner, thus making her available in the mating pool. Such a solution might serve the therapist's fitness goals (perhaps unconsciously) and not necessarily the patient's.

6.2 Religiosity and Faith

It is customary for a treatment rationale (conceptualization) to be presented to patients in the first sessions, after the initial assessments. The backbone idea of an evolutionary-driven intervention is the fact that humans are the product of evolution and that this simple and evident fact has enormous consequences on our behavior. How should a therapist approach a client who holds deep religious beliefs and who might consider Darwin's theory of evolution blasphemy?

It is important that in such a situation the therapist do not challenge deeply held religious beliefs, as this will significantly affect the treatment outcomes by decreasing the therapeutic alliance. For religious clients, the therapist should explain how humans are believed to have achieved reproductive success, citing relevant research on inclusive fitness and leaving aside the sensitive issue of whether humans are a product of evolution or not – which, in any case, would not be relevant for the actual treatment. For more inquisitive religious clients, the therapist can cite the theory of "intelligent design", which posits the role of a Creator, while not denying humans' relatedness to animals. Or s/he may cite Pope Francis, who stated that the theory of evolution is not incompatible with the existence of a Creator, but requires it ("Pope Francis declares evolution and Big Bang theory are real and God is not 'a magician with a magic wand' | The Independent," n.d.)

In short, the patient's religious beliefs should stay unchallenged. Generally, a safe approach is to present the framework of the interventions in a neutral way, insisting on empirical findings, not theoretical or philosophical abstractions. For instance, let's suppose we have a childless 55-year-old woman who is a devout Christian. In the case of a postmenopausal woman, one evolutionary-driven intervention may be to encourage her to maximize her *inclusive fitness* (Hamilton, 1964) by increasing her investment in relatives who carry copies of her genes (e.g., nephews, nieces, etcetera). The therapist, after describing the treatment rationale as explained above, could tell her that *"research has shown that women who are past a certain age – especially those who are post menopause – are less likely to become depressed if they maintain close and rich relationships with second- and third-degree younger relatives, such as nephews and nieces"* and devise an appropriate action plan in this direction.

In short, while the central assumption of an evolutionary-driven intervention is the fact that humans are the product of evolution, the main two ideas that can be inserted in the actual CET protocol need not challenge creationistic convictions. Firstly, patients of various denominations can easily accept the idea that the human cognitive system is adapted to an environment we lived in for almost our entire history. Secondly, patients will easily accept the truism that our ancestral environments were markedly different from the modern ones, and that this can have significant consequences on human psychology. Neither of these two assumptions challenges religious beliefs directly.

6.3 Patient's Sexual Orientation

Humans have evolved mechanisms designed to increase fitness, and these mechanisms' functions are those of survival and reproduction (i.e., finding suitable opposite-sex mates). An evolutionary therapist, however, might have a young homosexual client whose chances at direct reproductive success may be nil, so there cannot be interventions on this dimension.

The sensible therapeutic approach in such cases is to prescribe interventions along the dimensions of inclusive fitness (e.g., investing in genetic relatives), as well as interventions that increase mate value irrespective of the sexual orientation of the client. If one of the factors that makes this patient depressed is the patient's sexual orientation, the therapist can attempt to normalize it by citing evolutionary research showing that some gay men, for instance, are more likely to invest in blood relatives or that, in the past, homosexuals occupied high status in the society (e.g., nuns and monks), thus benefitting the family indirectly (Barash, 2012), therefore, from a genes' transmission point of view, they are actually no different from heterosexual men.

References

Bailey, K. G. (2000). Evolution, kinship, and psychotherapy: Promoting psychological health through human relationships. In P. Gilbert & K. G. Bailey (Eds.), *Genes on the couch: Explorations in evolutionary psychotherapy* (pp. 42–67). Hove, UK: Brunner-Routledge.

Barash, D. P. (2012). *Homo mysterious—Evolutionary puzzles of human nature*. New York, NY: Oxford University Press.

Buss, D. M. (2000). The evolution of happiness. *The American Psychologist, 55*(1), 15–23.

Gilbert, P., & Bailey, K. G. (Eds.). (2000). *Genes on the couch: Explorations in evolutionary psychotherapy*. Hove, UK: Brunner-Routledge.

Hamilton, W. D. (1964). The genetical evolution of social behavior. I and II. *Journal of Theoretical Biology, 7*, 1–52.

Kriegman, D. (2000). Evolutionary psychoanalysis: Toward an adaptive, biological perspective on the clinical process in psychoanalytic psychotherapy. In P. Gilbert & K. G. Bailey (Eds.), *Genes on a couch: Explorations in evolutionary psychotherapy* (pp. 71–92). Hove, UK: Brunner-Routledge.

Pope Francis declares evolution and Big Bang theory are real and God is not "a magician with a magic wand" | The Independent. (n.d.). Retrieved February 18, 2018, from The Independent website: http://www.independent.co.uk/news/world/europe/pope-francis-declares-evolution-and-big-bang-theory-are-right-and-god-isnt-a-magician-with-a-magic-9822514.html

Thornhill, R., & Palmer, C. T. (2000). *A natural history of rape: Biological bases of sexual coercion*. Cambridge, MA: The MIT Press.

Thornhill, R., & Palmer, C. T. (2004). Evolutionary life history perspective on rape. In *Evolutionary psychology, public policy and personal decisions* (pp. 249–274). Mahway, NJ: Lawrence Erlbaum.

Chapter 7
Specific Aspects Related to CET

7.1 Therapist's Background

Evolutionary psychotherapies stem directly from the tenets of evolutionary psychology. As such, a therapist who is providing this kind of interventions must be well versed in the theoretical aspects of evolutionary psychology. While formal advanced background in evolutionary psychology is not required, a good mastery of the fundamental concepts in this discipline is mandatory. The therapist can obtain this knowledge from handbooks such as David Buss's (2005) or introductory texts such as "Evolutionary Psychology: The New Science of the Mind" (Buss, 2015).

Also, the main methods in CET for depression are those also used in CBT (e.g. cognitive restructuring, behavioral activation), and, as such, a therapist with experience in CBT might find it easier to adapt than one specialized in other therapeutic approaches.

7.2 Psychotherapeutic Alliance

Close kinship relations – in their ideal manifestations – are warm, close, emphatic, giving, loving, and secure. During the time of our evolutionary history, we lived in tribal bands consisting of about 150 members (Dunbar, 1992), in which we knew each other well, and in which we were involved in complex group dynamics, such as mutual support and shared affection and resources, but also conflict and rivalry. In ancestral societies, biological and *psychological kinship* relations included warmth and love, as well as obligations and entitlements (Bailey, 2000). A "psychological kin" is a minimally related or unrelated individual who is integrated into the family circle, thus receiving rights and obligations which, although secondary to official biological kin, were true kin nevertheless – in other words, this person

C. Giosan, *Cognitive Evolutionary Therapy for Depression*, SpringerBriefs in Psychology, https://doi.org/10.1007/978-3-030-38874-4_7

received family status (Bailey, 2000; Bailey, Wood, & Nava, 1992). Some authors have argued that balanced and strong psychological and biological kinship relationships are linked to psychological health (Bailey, 2000).

Drawing on the above, the evolutionary therapist and the client should work in a warm, kin-like context, as opposed to the detached professionalism, or friendly neutrality, that characterizes other forms of therapy, such as psychoanalysis. The therapist should become the patient's "psychological kin" – a "buddy", a good friend – *while maintaining a set of safe boundaries* (Bailey, 2000).

In order to do this, the evolutionary therapist should go beyond the insights from REBT, where the therapeutic alliance centers on empathy, unconditional acceptance, genuineness, and humor (Bernard, 1991; David, Lynn, & Ellis, 2009; Ellis, Dryden, & DiGiuseppe, 2007; Walen, DiGiuseppe, & Dryden, 1992). On top of these very desirable therapist characteristics, the ability and willingness to make the extra-step of establishing a more personal relationship with the patient can be critical.

A note of caution: When building this relationship, the therapist should be mindful that different patients may perceive a therapist's attempt to establish rapport differently, so the therapist must navigate through this with great care. For example, abuse victims may perceive caring/closeness signals as a threat. Depressed patients might see a therapist's disclosure of his or her own personal problems as a signal that the therapist is too "weak to be of help." All these can greatly impact the establishment of rapport. Thus, to achieve optimal results with a depressed patient, the therapist must balance overt friendship versus reservation wisely.

Also, there may be the case that some patients might benefit more from an authoritative therapist (which would, evolutionarily speaking, tap into 'hierarchical' relationships), in which case more formality in the relationship might be beneficial. The therapist should use his or her clinical judgement to make such determinations on a case by case basis.

7.3 Decorum

The mismatch between our ancestral environments and the modern culture produces frustration and tension (Bailey, 1997; Crawford & Krebs, 1998). The overarching goal of an evolutionary-driven therapy is to reduce the gap between the traditional culture and the technology-based culture, and this can (and should) start with therapeutic setting itself.

For much of our pre-agricultural history, our ancestors were tribal groups of migrators. Therefore, the therapeutic setting should fit with this tendency of humans to search and explore. The therapeutic setting must be flexible, not rigid like the office settings that characterize many forms of modern therapy. Our ancestors did not stay in the same location with a friend for an hour every week for 3 months. On the contrary, they interacted in different settings and circumstances, and the evolutionary therapist must be creative and try to mimic those realities, to the extent that is possible. If local regulations permit (i.e., when liability is not an issue), the sessions can be conducted while walking in a park, sitting on a bench, or over a healthy meal in a quiet, green place. If the local regulations forbid this, then an occasional change in decorum (e.g., using another office in the same building for a couple of sessions) is recommended.

7.4 Behavioral Activation Versus CET for Depression

Because the dimensions of fitness differ as a function of gender/age of a person, an evolutionary-driven intervention is partially standardized (and customized) *a priori* for each patient. Unlike a standard behavioral approach, which draws heavily from Skinner's applied behavior analysis, evolutionary-based interventions stem from a paradigm that informs *beforehand* what specific behaviors should be encouraged or discouraged.

In behavioral activation, the intervention is generally directed at helping the patients to increase activation in such a way that they can experience greater contact with the sources of reward. To this end, behavioral activation includes analyses of behavior that help in the identification of the sources of reward.

In contrast, in an evolutionary-based intervention the identification of the sources of reward is guided by the evolutionary theory, so the therapist comes pre-equipped with a list of potential sources of fitness problems and opportunities for intervention. This general list is operationalized comprehensively by a measure called *The Evolutionary Fitness Scale – EFS* (Giosan, Wyka, Mogoaşe, Cobeanu, & Szentagotai, 2018) (EFS, see Appendix 1), which the patient completes *at the beginning* of treatment. The patient's answers to the EFS guide the therapeutic interventions (more on the EFS in the next sections).

In short, CET enhances the classic approach in cognitive-behavioral therapy by (1) focusing on specific, fitness-related problems, some of which might have never been freely recognized by the patient, and (2) by using a specialized evolutionary-aware conceptualization that enhances the effectiveness of CBT by normalizing expectations.

Like in classical CBT, at the beginning of the treatment the psychotherapist and the patient select and define the list of problems that will be addressed during therapy. However, unlike the standard CBT, these problems are primarily identified from the patient's answers to the Evolutionary Fitness Scale at intake (see Appendix 1).

Furthermore, in line with the evolutionary framing of the intervention, the therapist should note that fitness-related problems can have a high impact on quality of life and depressive symptomatology reduction, and will cite relevant research, some of which detailed in earlier in this manual. The therapist will use an evolutionary rationale to suggest that these fitness-related problems be prioritized. The therapist will also have an input on prioritizing the resolution of certain fitness-related problems over others, while giving the patient the latitude to make the final decision.

After the generation of the fitness-problem list as captured by the Evolutionary Fitness Scale, the therapist will elaborate the specific evolutionary conceptualizations of the patient's particular set of problems. In other words, besides the general CBT conceptualization, the therapist will include explanations about the distal causes of depression as applicable to that patient. This will help put the disorder in context, create a feeling of prediction and control regarding the treatment outcome, and reduce secondary problems related to the depressive symptoms (e.g., anxiety about depression, anger about depression or depression about feeling depressed).

Besides standard cognitive, behavioral and emotive techniques, discussions about human nature from an evolutionary standpoint (where appropriate, see the section on ethical aspects), will encourage the patient to experience acceptance (a key therapeutic ingredient) by acknowledging basic human limitations as well as strengths in oneself (self-acceptance), partner, family members or friends (other-acceptance) and the world in general (world-acceptance).

Furthermore, the evolutionary roots of our cognitive systems can be used as arguments for why people do not act or think as they "should". Such evolutionary arguments can become powerful tools in the disputing process, commonly used in standard cognitive therapies. Evolutionary-inspired concepts such as cognitive modularity, parental investment theory, conspicuous consumption and costly signaling theory, deference modules, moralistic judgment modules and hypocrisy (explained in layman's terms) can offer useful explanations for seemingly "aberrant" behaviors of self or others.

Besides addressing existing problems, towards the end of therapy the therapist may choose to address the patient's potential future fitness problems. The Mismatch Hypothesis (Lloyd, Wilson, & Sober, 2011) can inform and explain difficulties such as sticking with long-term plans, procrastination, difficulties with long-term relationships, etcetera, and the therapist should raise these potential problems (and offer possible solutions solutions) on a case-by-case basis as a relapse prevention and personal optimization measure.

7.5 Demographic-Related Interventions

As mentioned in the previous sections, and detailed further later, Cognitive Evolutionary Therapy for depression relies heavily on a *fitness evaluation* that takes place at intake, using the Evolutionary Fitness Scale (Giosan et al., 2018), which guides the subsequent interventions. However, the answers to this evaluation of a patient's fitness should be used in conjunction with the patient's *demographic* characteristics, because these characteristics can have a differential bearing on fitness.

For example, let's suppose we have two patients: a woman in her 50's (she can only increase her fitness indirectly, through investment in family members), and a man in his 50's (he can potentially achieve both direct and indirect fitness). Let's also suppose that both score low on EFS items tapping into personal attractiveness (i.e., direct fitness) and on investments in relatives (i.e., indirect fitness). The theoretical arguments presented in this manual suggest that interventions on dimensions that have effects on direct fitness in the case of the female patient will be less impactful than those that can increase this patient's indirect fitness, while in the case of the male patient both types of interventions might be equally effective and should be considered equally in treatment.

In short, demographic characteristics are very important because they provide a general framework that should be used in conjunction with the patient's answers to the EFS. Generally, a therapist should place emphasis on direct fitness (e.g., attractiveness, resource acquisition, mating) in patients of reproductive age and on indirect fitness in patients past their reproductive ages. Given the fact, however, that men's reproductive period is much longer than women's – a man can potentially reproduce throughout his entire lifetime – a therapist should use her clinical judgement for the most appropriate fitness interventions in such cases.

References

Bailey, K. G. (1997). Series on mismatch theory and the fourfold model. *ASCAP Newsletter*, (February, March, April, December).

Bailey, K. G. (2000). Evolution, kinship, and psychotherapy: Promoting psychological health through human relationships. In P. Gilbert & K. G. Bailey (Eds.), *Genes on the couch: Explorations in evolutionary psychotherapy* (pp. 42–67). Hove, UK: Brunner-Routledge.

Bailey, K. G., Wood, H. E., & Nava, G. R. (1992). What do clients want? Role of psychological kinship in professional helping. *Journal of Psychotherapy Integration, 2*(2), 125–147.

Bernard, M. E. (1991). *Using rational-emotive therapy effectively: A Practitioner's guide*. New York, NY: Springer.

Buss, D. M. (2005). *The handbook of evolutionary psychology*. Hoboken, NJ: Wiley.

Buss, D. M. (2015). *Evolutionary psychology: The new science of the mind* (5th ed.). Abingdon, OX: Routledge.

Crawford, C., & Krebs, D. (1998). *Handbook of evolutionary psychology: Ideas, issues, and applications*. Mahwah, NJ: Lawrence Erlbaum Associates, Inc.

David, D., Lynn, S. J., & Ellis, A. (Eds.). (2009). *Rational and irrational beliefs: Research, theory, and clinical practice*. New York, NY: Oxford University Press.

Dunbar, R. I. (1992). Neocortex size as a constraint on group size in primates. *Journal of Human Evolution, 22*(6), 469–493.

Ellis, A., Dryden, W., & DiGiuseppe, R. (2007). *The practice of rational emotive behavior therapy*. New York, NY: Springer.

Giosan, C., Wyka, K., Mogoaşe, C., Cobeanu, O., & Szentagotai, A. (2018). The Evolutionary Fitness scale: A measure of the independent criterion of fitness. *EvoS Journal: The Journal of the Evolutionary Studies Consortium, 7*(1), 181–205.

Lloyd, E., Wilson, D. S., & Sober, E. (2011). Evolutionary mismatch and what to do about it: A basic tutorial. *Evolutionary Applications*, 2–4.

Walen, S. R., DiGiuseppe, R., & Dryden, W. (1992). *A practitioner's guide to rational-emotive therapy*. Retrieved from http://books.google.ro/books?id=wH-YiZnJgB8C

Chapter 8
The Evolutionary Fitness Scale

As mentioned earlier, Cognitive Evolutionary Therapy for Depression starts with the administration of a fitness evaluation at intake. This instrument is called "The Evolutionary Fitness Scale" (Giosan, Wyka, Mogoașe, Cobeanu, & Szentagotai, 2018) and consists of 45 items (58 if the respondent has children) scored on a 1–5 Likert scale (see Fig. 8.1 for the English version and Fig. 8.2 for the Romanian version of this instrument). The items tap into dimensions that are thought to be implicated in reproductive success, some of which are health, attractiveness, safety of, and fit with the environment, resourcefulness, upward social mobility, reciprocal altruism, mate value, offspring quality, extended family. The patient's answers to this instrument guide the subsequent evolutionary interventions, which can be behavioral activation or cognitive restructuring targeting the patient's fitness deficiencies.

Let's illustrate this through several examples of EFS items, assuming a hypothetical patient who has stated disagreement.

- EFS item: "*I am not afraid of intrusions or burglaries in the house I live*". This item taps on safety of the environment. The therapist should initiate a conversation to address this problem, and, together with the patient, come up with some potential solutions (e.g., an alarm system, more secure locks, a guard dog, etcetera).
- EFS items: "*I often get the chance to spend time outside*" and "*I am an active outdoors person*". These items tap into (mis)fits with the environment. People generally report higher levels of well-being when they spend time in nature. After ruling out potential health problems that might prevent a patient from spending time outdoors, the therapist should initiate a conversation for a concrete plan for the patient to do that (e.g., hiking, walking in parks, etc.). Like in standard cognitive approaches, the patient should be given "homework" to this effect.

C. Giosan, *Cognitive Evolutionary Therapy for Depression*, SpringerBriefs in Psychology, https://doi.org/10.1007/978-3-030-38874-4_8

1. I have at least one best friend.

2. In general, my extended family members, especially my first-degree relatives, have enjoyed great longevity.

3. I have many friends ready to help me in case of need.

4. I eat very healthy.

5. I have significant medical problems.

6. I may not be a millionaire, but I make enough money to afford many of the things I want.

7. People find me sexually attractive.

8. I engage in activities, at my job or elsewhere, that put my life at risk.

9. I am generally satisfied with my sex life.

10. My health coverage is enough to pay for any unexpected medical bills.

11. I visit my relatives frequently.

12. I am not afraid of intrusions or burglaries in the house I live.

13. I often get the chance to spend time outside.

14. I am more attractive to potential sexual partners than the majority of my peers.

15. I am an active outdoors person.

16. I get to tend to pets and animals often.

17. I like to gather wild strawberries and other edible things from nature when given the opportunity.

18. I eat at least three servings of vegetables or fruits per day.

19. I eat nuts frequently.

20. I eat plenty of fish.

Fig. 8.1 The Evolutionary Fitness Scale (EFS). (Giosan et al., 2018) (English version)
Author's note: This instrument may be reproduced and used for non-commercial research and educational purposes without seeking written permission. Distribution must be controlled, meaning only to the participants engaged in the research or enrolled in the educational activity. Any other type of reproduction, distribution, or use of this instrument, such as administering it to clients in private practice, is not authorized without written permission from the author and publisher

21. I get enough sleep.

22. Most of the days I eat lean meats (e.g., chicken breast) rather than fat cuts.

23. I exercise at least four times a week.

24. I am in a better physical shape than the majority of people my age.

25. I am not afraid to walk at night in my neighborhood.

26. I have the ability to protect me and my family in case of natural disasters or accidents (e.g., flood, fire).

27. I would find a date easily, if I wanted to.

28. I frequently go out with my friends.

29. I fit well with my coworkers or schoolmates.

30. The circumstances in which I find myself now are a good match with my personal goals and aspirations.

31. I fit well with my neighbors.

32. My family members brag about me.

33. I am admired by my friends.

34. I help many people.

35. I am important to people other than my family.

36. My friends contact me often.

37. My family contact me often.

38. I believe people find my partner more attractive than the majority of his/her peers.

39. I am satisfied with my sex life with my partner.

Fig. 8.1 (continued)

40. My partner and I are very compatible sexually.

41. I believe my partner is faithful to me.

42. My partner enjoys good health.

43. I have a harmonious, conflict-free, relationship with my partner.

44. If I made no money, I could rely on my partner's income for a while without a significant drop in my quality of life.

45. If I wanted to, my partner would have a child with me.

If you have children, please fill out the following items:

46. My relatives would take care of my children, in case of need.

47. My children are better at sports than the majority of their peers.

48. My children are in top 10% at school.

49. I could count on my close friends to take care of my children in case of need.

50. My children rarely get sick.

51. People say my children are very cute.

52. I am pleased with my child's boyfriend/girlfriend selection.

53. I have a close relationship with my children.

54. My children's ideas often irritate me.

55. My children confide in me.

56. I get into frequent arguments with my children.

57. I don't like my children's friends.

58. My children trust and follow my advice.

Fig. 8.1 (continued)

1. Am cel puţin un prieten foarte bun.

2. În general, rudele mele, în special cele apropiate, au trăit mult.

3. Am mulți prieteni gata să mă ajute în caz de nevoie.

4. Mănânc foarte sănătos.

5. Am probleme mari de sănătate.

6. Chiar dacă nu sunt foarte bogat(ă), fac destui bani ca să îmi permit multe din lucrurile pe care mi le doresc.

7. Cred că oamenii mă consideră atractiv(ă).

8. Am o meserie sau fac activităţi care îmi pun viaţa în pericol.

9. În general sunt satisfăcut(ă) de viaţa mea sexuală.

10. Am acces la servicii medicale de bună calitate.

11. Îmi vizitez rudele frecvent.

12. Nu îmi este frică de intruziuni sau tâlhării în casa în care locuiesc.

13. Am de multe ori şansa să îmi petrec timpul în aer liber.

14. Sunt mai atractiv(ă) sexual decât majoritatea celorlalţi de vârsta mea.

15. Sunt o persoană activă, care iese în natură.

16. Am des ocazia să îngrijesc sau să mă joc cu animale.

17. Îmi place să culeg fragi sau alte fructe din natură, atunci când am posibilitatea.

18. Mănânc cel puţin trei porţii de vegetale sau fructe pe zi.

19. Consum frecvent nuci şi seminţe.

20. Mănânc mult peşte.

21. Dorm suficient.

Fig. 8.2 The Evolutionary Fitness Scale (EFS). (Giosan et al., 2018) (Romanian version)

22. De obicei mănânc carne slabă (de ex. piept de pui) şi nu grăsimi.

23. Fac exerciţii fizice cel puţin de patru ori pe săptămână.

24. Sunt într-o formă fizică mai bună decât majoritatea celorlalţi oameni de vârstamea.

25. Nu mi-e teamă să merg noaptea pe stradă în zona în care locuiesc.

26. În caz de pericol neprevăzut (de exemplu: inundaţie, incendiu), pot să mă protejez pe mine şi pe familia mea.

27. Dacă aş dori, mi-ar fi uşor să îmi găsesc un nou partener romantic.

28. Ies des cu prietenii mei.

29. Mă potrivesc cu colegii mei de şcoală sau de muncă.

30. În prezent, punctul în care mă aflu în viaţa mea se potriveşte cu scopurile şi aspiraţiile mele.

31. Mă simt bine în comunitatea în care trăiesc.

32. Familia mea se laudă cu mine.

33. Prietenii mei mă admiră.

34. Ajut mulţi oameni.

35. Sunt important(ă) şi pentru alţi oameni, nu doar pentru familia mea.

36. Prietenii mei mă contactează des.

37. Membrii familiei mele mă contactează des.

38. Cred că oamenii consideră că persoana care îmi este partner(ă) este mai atractivă decât majoritatea celorlalţi de vârsta ei.

39. Sunt satisfacut(ă) de viaţa mea sexuală cu partenerul/partenera mea.

40. Eu şi partenerul/partenera mea ne potrivim foarte bine din punct de vedere sexual.

41. Cred că partenerul/partenera mea îmi este fidel(ă).

42. Partenerul/partenera mea nu are probleme mari de sănătate.

Fig. 8.2 (continued)

43. Am o relație de cuplu armonioasă, fără conflicte.

44. Dacă nu aş lucra, aş putea să mă bazez pentru o vreme pe venitul partenerului/partnerei, fără să simt o scădere semnificativă a calității vieții mele.

45. Dacă aş dori, partenerul/partenera mea ar face un copil cu mine.

Dacă aveți copii completați următoarele:

46. Rudele mele ar avea grijă de copiii mei, dacă aş avea nevoie.

47. Copiii mei sunt mai buni la sport decât majoritatea celor de vârsta lor.

48. Copiii mei sunt printre primii din clasă la învățătură.

49. Dacă ar fi nevoie ca cineva să aibă grijă de copiii mei, m-aş putea baza pe prietenii mei.

50. Copiii mei se îmbolnăvesc rar.

51. Oamenii apreciază cât de frumoşi sunt copiii mei.

52. Sunt mulțumit(ă) de partenerul romantic al copilului meu.

53. Am o relație apropiată cu copiii mei.

54. Ideile copiilor mei mă irită adesea.

55. Copiii mei mi se destăinuie.

56. Mă cert deseori cu copiii mei.

57. Nu îmi plac prietenii copiilor mei.

58. Copiii mei au încredere în sfaturile mele şi le urmează.

Fig. 8.2 (continued)

Unlike standard cognitive approaches, however, this behavioral activation element was not generated by the patient in therapy but was captured *a priori* at intake by the EFS.

- EFS item: "*I frequently go out with my friends*". This item taps into social capital and reciprocal altruism. Having many friends who can help a person in case of need (e.g., by babysitting a child) can have a positive impact on fitness. The therapist should work with the patient by making concrete plans for the patient to meet friends regularly/more often.
- EFS item: "*I am satisfied by my sex life with my partner*". If the patient does not have a partner, the therapist will begin a conversation to pinpoint the root of the problem, then come up with potential strategies, on a case by case basis. If the patient does have a partner, the therapist should initiate a conversation to pinpoint the cause of the sexual inactivity (e.g., sexual incompatibility, boredom, etc.) and discuss possible solutions.

In most of the cases, the fitness problems captured by the EFS can be addressed in therapy. In some cases, however, some of the problems indicated by a patient's answers to the EFS are not addressable. For instance, a patient might answer negatively at the EFS item "*I visit my relatives frequently*" because she might not have relatives, or because her relatives live on a different continent. In such a case, very little can be done along this dimension and the therapist should focus on the other fitness problems indicated by the EFS.

Furthermore, a patient's answers at the EFS will typically reveal many fitness areas that need improvement. In some cases, it is not practical to work on all of them, because of logistical constraints or time. In such situations, the therapist should rank these fitness problems in terms of their likely impact on fitness (e.g., lack of a partner has a greater impact on fitness than not having the possibility to tend to pets and animals often) and work on the more fitness-relevant ones first.

Reference

Giosan, C., Wyka, K., Mogoașe, C., Cobeanu, O., & Szentagotai, A. (2018). The Evolutionary Fitness scale: A measure of the independent criterion of fitness. *EvoS Journal: The Journal of the Evolutionary Studies Consortium, 7*(1), 181–205.

Chapter 9
The General Structure of CET and Examples of Evolutionary Interventions

What follows in the next pages is a structured therapy protocol of the Cognitive Evolutionary Therapy. It is based on a protocol tested in a randomized clinical trial that compared it to Cognitive Therapy (Giosan et al., 2014; Giosan, Muresan, & Moldovan, 2014), but expands on it by incorporating, besides specific cognitive techniques, elements specific to Rational Emotive Behavior Therapy (REBT). Therapists should use their clinical judgment in deciding whether to follow the REBT enriched protocol presented below, or the original one, or variations.

At the end of this chapter, examples of possible interventions on each of the items from the Evolutionary Fitness Scale (Giosan et al. 2018) are also given (see Fig. 9.1).

The standard CET intervention consists of 12 individual 60-min therapy sessions, whose structure is presented below. However, the evolutionary therapist is free to adapt and adjust the number of sessions as she sees fit.

Like in classical CBT, the therapy sessions are highly structured. They generally start by setting an agenda listing the items to be dealt with during the session. The patient and the therapist agree on the contents of the agenda, which always includes a review of the previous week's homework, along with one or two specific problems that will be the main focus of the session.

The sessions should therefore follow this format:

- Brief update and mood check
- Bridge from previous session
- Set agenda
- Review homework
- Potential supporting exercises
- Summary
- Assign homework
- Feedback

C. Giosan, *Cognitive Evolutionary Therapy for Depression*, SpringerBriefs in Psychology, https://doi.org/10.1007/978-3-030-38874-4_9

	Item	Broad evolutionary factor(s) tapped	Some suggestions for therapy Note: wherever appropriate, therapy targets both behavioral activation and correction of dysfunctional thinking
1.	I have at least one best friend	Direct fitness	- If patient can't name a best friend, explore reasons and refute dysfunctional thinking. - Explore modalities to increase connectedness with at least one non-relative.
2.	In general, my extended family members, especially my first-degree relatives, have enjoyed great longevity	Indirect fitness	- Determine the factors that led to decreased longevity. If accidents/disasters/wars, etc., don't insist. - If illnesses, discuss if better health care/preventative care is needed and ways to achieve that.
3.	I have many friends ready to help me in case of need	Direct fitness	- Patient is encouraged to join groups such as churches, volunteer organizations, social groups (e.g., hobby groups). - Solutions such as meetup should be explored.
4.	I eat very healthy	Direct fitness Mismatch	- See item 18.
5.	I don't have major medical problems	Direct fitness	- Explore ways to correct some of the problems (e.g., doctor referrals, healthier lifestyle) where appropriate.
6.	I may not be a millionaire, but I make enough money to afford many of the things I want	Direct fitness Indirect fitness	- Explore solutions to increase the chance of making more money (e.g., furthering education, a business venture/partnership, acquiring new skills, etcetera).

Fig. 9.1 Examples of evolutionary inspired interventions, based on the Evolutionary Fitness Scale (Giosan et al., 2018)
Author's note: This instrument may be reproduced and used for non-commercial research and educational purposes without seeking written permission. Distribution must be controlled, meaning only to the participants engaged in the research or enrolled in the educational activity. Any other type of reproduction, distribution, or use of this instrument, such as administering it to clients in private practice, is not authorized without written permission from the author and publisher

7.	People find me sexually attractive	Direct fitness	- Discuss ways to increase attractiveness (e.g., clothes, hairdos, makeup, posture, demeanor). - Discuss what attractiveness means for the client. - Change self-perceptions.
8.	I engage in activities, at my job or elsewhere, that put my life at risk	Direct fitness	- Consider sex differences. Women are more risk-averse than men. - In therapy with male patients, an analysis of the cost-benefits of the risk should be made. - In therapy with female patients, ways to reduce the risk of those activities will be discussed/explored if the patient so desires.
9.	I am generally satisfied with my sex life	Direct fitness	- If appropriate, normalize expectations by presenting the average number of times people of various ages have sex. - If the patient has a partner, discuss the reasons for the incompatibility. The patient might need sex/couple therapy.
10.	My health coverage is enough to pay for any unexpected medical bills	Direct fitness	- Explore ways to better network with doctors and identify good and affordable health clinics.
11.	I visit my relatives frequently	Indirect fitness	- Explore solutions for more frequent contact with family members. - If distance is an issue, explore virtual solutions (e.g., Skype).
12.	I am not afraid of intrusions or burglaries in the house I live.	Direct fitness	- Explore solutions to increase home security (e.g., alarm system, guard dog, etcetera)
13.	I often get the chance to spend time outside	Mismatch	- If permanent relocation to "greener places" is not an option, ways to be in closer touch with nature will be explored (e.g., hiking, trips "off the beaten path," parks, etc.)

Fig. 9.1 (continued)

14.	I am more attractive to potential sexual partners than the majority of my peers	Direct fitness	- See item 7.
15.	I am an active outdoors person	Mismatch	- See item 13.
16.	I get to tend to pets and animals often	Mismatch	- Discuss ways to be in closer touch with animals (e.g. bird feeding in parks). - Explore the possibility of buying (or borrowing) a pet. - Suggests visit to the zoo or animal farms. - Suggest visits to friends who own pets.
17.	I like to gather wild strawberries and other edible things from nature when given the opportunity	Mismatch	- Discuss/explore solutions for a more active hunter/gatherer lifestyle (e.g., mushrooms picking after rain / wild strawberries / apple picking).
18.	I eat at least three servings of vegetables or fruits per day	Direct fitness Mismatch	- Explain the basic premises of a hunter-gatherer diet, and how this diet is generally associated with positive health outcomes (Therapist should be familiar with Loren Cordain's works). - Ask that the patient get clearance from a general practitioner to transition towards a diet richer in lean meats/nuts/veggies/fruits and poorer in processed carbohydrates like white bread, sugar, dairy products. - Develop concrete plans as appropriate. - See Appendix 1
19.	I eat nuts frequently	Mismatch	- See item 18.
20.	I eat plenty of fish	Mismatch	- See item 18.
21.	I get enough sleep	Direct fitness Mismatch	- Determine the barriers to getting enough sleep, besides depression.

Fig. 9.1 (continued)

			- Discuss alternatives/solutions to achieve ~8 hours of sleep per day.
22.	Most of the days I eat lean meats (e.g., chicken breast) rather than fat cuts.	Mismatch	- See item 18.
23.	I exercise at least four times a week	Direct fitness Mismatch	- See item 24.
24.	I am in a better physical shape than the majority of people my age.	Direct fitness	- Set up plans to get in better shape (e.g., gym subscription). - Set up plans to hire a personal trainer, if adequate. - Ask the patient to get a doctor's clearance for increased physical activity. - Instruct the patient to engage in social physical activities over lonely ones (e.g., team games like basketball or volleyball).
25.	I am not afraid to walk at night in my neighborhood.	Direct fitness	- Explore solutions. Is moving to a different neighborhood feasible? - If patient works night shifts, is a schedule change feasible? - If local regulations permit, explore the possibility of defense solutions (e.g., pepper spray). - If appropriate, explore the possibility of taking up defense classes (this would tap into items 23 and 24 as well).
26.	I have the ability to protect me and my family in case of natural disasters or accidents (e.g., flood, fire).	Direct fitness Indirect fitness	- Ask patient if s/he has ever thought of emergency plans. - Explore various emergency plans. - Instruct the patient to conduct emergency drills.
27.	I would find a date easily, if I wanted to.	Direct fitness	- Address the psychological obstacles involved in finding a date first (e.g., approach anxiety, low self-esteem, negative body language).

Fig. 9.1 (continued)

			- Explore ways for the patient to be in greater contact with potential partners (e.g., joining social groups sharing a hobby, going out more often, meetups, relocation, etcetera). - Decide on some solutions and work with the patient to implement them.
28.	I frequently go out with my friends.	Direct fitness Mismatch	- Explore the barriers (e.g., scheduling conflicts, workload, lack of motivation). - Discuss solutions and work on their implementation in the form of homework.
29.	I fit well with my coworkers	Mismatch	- Explore ways to correct the problem (e.g., job change).
30.	The circumstances in which I find myself now are a good match with my personal goals and aspirations	Direct fitness	- Make concrete initial plans to change circumstances, if necessary. - Set deadlines.
31.	I fit well with my neighbors	Mismatch	- Explore solutions (e.g., moving to a different area).
32.	My family members brag about me	Direct fitness Indirect fitness	- Discuss solutions to increase status (e.g., more education if appropriate, job change, community involvement, etcetera).
33.	I am admired by my friends	Direct fitness	- Discuss the psychological aspects of establishing and maintaining friendships and admiration from others (e.g., good communication, assertiveness, active listening skills, empathy and emotional intelligence). - Explore ways to increase status and own importance (e.g., furthering education, business ventures, physical attractiveness). - Explore ways to capitalize on patient's unique assets and skills by joining groups that value them (Tooby & Cosmides, 1990).

Fig. 9.1 (continued)

34.	I help many people	Direct fitness Reciprocal Altruism	- Therapist works with patient to develop a caring mentality (attitude) along with concrete plans for helping others.
35.	I am important to people other than my family	Direct fitness	- See item 33.
36.	My friends contact me often	Direct fitness	- Therapist encourages the patient to take initiative and get in touch with friends. Therapist also instructs the patient to ask his/her friends to contact him/her regularly - Patient is encouraged to disclose their problem with friends but discouraged to spend too much time talking about depression. Time should be spent on shared social activities. - Ask the patient for permission to work with the patient's friends (to the extent this is possible/appropriate), to increase contact with the patient. - Ask the patient to keep a log of these activities and intervene as necessary
37.	My family contact me often	Direct fitness Indirect fitness	- Ask the patient to instruct his/her family members to get in touch with him more often. Instruct the patient to talk about his/her problems with the family, while avoiding ruminating. - Ask the patient for permission to work with the patient's immediate family (to the extent this is possible/appropriate), to increase contact with the patient (approach somewhat similar to that in the Behavioral Activation Treatment for Depression). - Ask the patient to keep a log of weekly contacts. Ask the family members to increase contact if still necessary.

Fig. 9.1 (continued)

			- Instruct the patient (or family) to engage in shared activities, rather than in discussions about the patient's depression. Instruct the patient to disclose about his/her problems, but not to ruminate about them with family.
38.	I believe people find my partner more attractive than the majority of his/her peers.	Direct fitness	- Analyze what "attractiveness" means for the patient. - Analyze what the importance of others' assessments in this regard is for the patient. - Discuss ways to make the patient's partner more attractive (e.g., clothing, hairdos, physical shape, etc.). The patient should play an active role in this. Therapist must show great sensitivity in intervening on the third party.
39.	I am satisfied with my sex life with my partner.	Direct fitness	- See item 9.
40.	My partner and I are very compatible sexually	Direct fitness	- See item 9.
41.	I believe my partner is faithful to me	Direct fitness	- Discuss with great sensitivity.
42.	My partner enjoys good health	Direct fitness	- Analyze and discuss the seriousness of the problems, and possible solutions. - Address psychological barriers to medical treatment, such as procrastination of checkups, avoidance, or inefficient communication with the partner.
43.	I have a harmonious, conflict-free, relationship with my partner	Direct fitness	- Analyze sources of conflict. - Discuss solutions. - Refer patient to couple's therapy after the end of current treatment, if necessary.

Fig. 9.1 (continued)

44.	If I made no money, I could rely on my partner's income for a while without a significant drop in my quality of life	Direct fitness	- Discuss/explore backup financial planning that would help in case of need. - Refer the patient to a financial planner, if necessary
45.	If I wanted to, my partner would have a child with me	Direct fitness.	- Discuss, if appropriate, the reasons why having children is not an option at the moment. - Explore solutions and planning (e.g., job stability, flextime, financial planning, family planning, etc.)
46.	My relatives would take care of my children, in case of need	Direct fitness	- Explore ways to be in closer contact with family members, if possible. - See item 11.
47.	My children are better at sports than the majority of their peers	Direct fitness	- Discuss ways to send the patient's children to sports. - Make concrete plans and establish deadlines.
48.	My children are in top 10% at school	Direct fitness	- Make plans to improve academic performance (e.g., tutoring, spending more time with the child's homework, etc.) - Adhere to the solutions proposed.
49.	I could count on my close friends to take care of my children in case of need	Direct fitness	- See items 1 and 3.
50.	My children don't get sick often	Direct fitness	- Discuss ways to make the patient's children stronger (e.g., healthy eating habits, sports, etcetera).
51.	People say my children are very cute	Direct fitness	- See item 47.
52.	I am pleased with my child's boyfriend/girlfriend selection	Indirect fitness	- Discuss perceptions - Discuss intergenerational conflict - Discuss solutions/strategies

Fig. 9.1 (continued)

53.	I have a close relationship with my children	Direct fitness	- Explore the reasons for the relationship problem. - Explore solutions.
54.	My children's ideas often irritate me	Direct fitness	- See item 53.
55.	My children confide in me	Direct fitness	- See item 53.
56.	I get into frequent arguments with my children	Direct fitness	- See item 53.
57.	I don't like my children's friends	Direct fitness	- See item 52.
58.	My children trust and follow my advice	Direct fitness	- See item 53.

Fig. 9.1 (continued)

9.1 Session 1

The first session starts with a general discussion about depression – what it is, what consequences it can have, what treatments exist. It also focuses on educating the patient about psychotherapy, emphasizing the importance of "homework" (personal practice of the therapy at home), taking responsibility for change, and adjusting the patient's expectations.

This first session will also consist of an explanation of the broad premises of the evolutionary-based intervention (being mindful of the ethical issues outlined earlier in this manual). The therapist will explain that the current approaches to depression view it as a brain disorder, but that recent research points to the fact that depression, at least mild to moderate, can be an adaptive mechanism signaling reproductive costs or problems, and that many of these problems are captured by the Evolutionary Fitness Scale, which the patient completed at intake. The goal of the therapy, the patient is further explained, is to find solutions to (some of) these problems and/or to correct irrational beliefs linked to them. According to research, the patient is told, when adequate solutions to these problems are found, depression is likely to subside.

This session also focuses on presenting more detailed explanations about the evolutionary causes of depression, such as the mismatch theory (the theory that cognitive structures which were adaptive in a Pleistocene environment, but are now 'mismatched' to the current environment, leading to dysfunctional emotions and behaviors), and about some of the hypothesized evolutionary functions of depression (Nesse & Williams, 1994). The patient is also informed in this session about the research linking depression and fitness-related behaviors, and why an evolutionary approach is suitable as a guiding add-on to a cognitive intervention. This is also the point where the therapist discusses the problems identified by the EFS at intake and, with the help of the patient, sets realistic goals to address them in future sessions. The homework in this session usually consists of building specific goals, using the EFS as a guideline and as an example of specific target behaviors.

Structurally, session 1 includes:

- Setting the agenda (and providing a rationale for doing so);
- Doing a mood check, including objective scores;
- Beginning the development of the therapeutic relationship;
- Educating the patient about psychotherapy (emphasizing the importance of homework and taking responsibility for change) and specific CET insights (mismatch theory, depression as adaptation, etc.);
- Briefly reviewing the presenting problems and obtaining an update (since evaluation);
- Discussion about the problems identified by the EFS and setting goals;
- Eliciting and adjusting the patients' expectations for therapy;
- Educating the patient about depression;
- Setting the homework;
- Providing a summary;
- Giving and eliciting feedback.

9.2 Session 2

Session 2 focuses on continuing to build the therapeutic alliance and elaborating on the fitness problems revealed by EFS. This session also provides the opportunity to discuss the patient's understanding of the distal/evolutionary causes of depression.

Structurally, session 2 includes:

- Continuation of the construction of the therapeutic relationship;
- Elaborating the problem list generated by the EFS;
- Homework suggestions:
  - Self-monitoring of depression and anxiety symptoms;
  - EFS-generated behavioral activation (i.e., homework targeted at solving some problems identified by the EFS);
  - Monitoring of previous coping strategies with depression.

9.3 Sessions 3–6

Sessions 3–6 focus on working on each of the fitness deficiencies identified by EFS at intake (see Fig. 9.1). These problems are conceptualized using evolutionary insights. For instance, some dysfunctional beliefs and their consequences can be seen as adaptive mental structures left over from the Environment of Evolutionary Adaptedness (Irons, 1998). This helps the patient to begin to experience control and self-acceptance of their depressive symptoms. For example, a patient can present guilt – a symptom of depression – about feelings or expressions of anger, fueled by beliefs such as: "I'm a horrible person because I got angry and yelled at my neighbor." In such a case, guilt is typically seen as a secondary emotional problem, that is, a dysfunctional emotion about other emotions (Ellis, Dryden, & DiGiuseppe, 2007). Evolutionary explanations of anger (for example, anger as an adaptive reaction during the EEA) can lower self-criticism and promote self-acceptance by reducing the intensity of the secondary emotion (guilt in this example), thus enabling the psychotherapist to work on the primary, present problem (anger in this example).

Homework is negotiated during these sessions and generally consists of self-monitoring of emotions and behaviors, cognitive restructuring, and behavioral activation tasks generated from the EFS. Specific behaviors that the patient is not engaging in as captured by the EFS (for example, spending time in nature, exercise, healthy eating habits) are targeted for activation (see Appendices 1 and 2). In addition, problem-solving, conflict resolution, and assertiveness training are used to enhance relationships with the patient's relatives where appropriate, thus tapping into indirect fitness, while direct fitness (for example, mate value, health, income) is enhanced with standard CT techniques.

Structurally, sessions 3–6 include:

- Working on each problem generated by the EFS, and generated by the patient, based on the ABCDE model;
- Conceptualizing and reframing problems according to the insights from evolutionary psychology;
- Working toward strengthening the patients' rational beliefs and weakening the irrational beliefs;
- Encouraging the patients to see the links between problems, particularly those which are characterized by common irrational beliefs.
- Homework suggestions:
  - EFS-generated behavioral activation;
  - Emotion control by cognitive restructuring when prone to depressive symptoms;
  - Self-monitoring while using cognitive restructuring techniques in imagined situations;
  - Self-monitoring while using cognitive restructuring techniques in real life situations;
  - Rehearsal of relaxation exercises.

9.4 Sessions 7–10

Sessions 7–10 are targeted at making headways towards the resolution of some or all the problems previously identified by the EFS, working toward strengthening the patients' adaptive beliefs and weakening the maladaptive ones, and encouraging them to see the links between problems, particularly those that are characterized by common dysfunctional beliefs. Core beliefs are identified and approached in this part of the therapy. Standard CT techniques are used to change beliefs and behaviors, but the therapist often refers back to the evolutionary-informed CT conceptualization. Homework continues to focus on EFS-generated behavioral activation, rehearsing adaptive statements in real-life situations and applying the techniques and conceptualization to novel, diverse problems.

Structurally, sessions 7–10 include:

- Making headways towards the resolution of all or some of the problems previously identified by the EFS;
- Working toward strengthening the patients' adaptive beliefs and weakening the maladaptive beliefs;
- Encourage the patients to see the links between problems, particularly those which are characterized by common irrational beliefs;
- Homework suggestions:
  - Continuing EFS-generated behavioral activation;
  - Rehearsing rational statements in real life situations;
  - Use cognitive conceptualization to deal with negative emotions related to depression.

9.5 Sessions 11–12

Sessions 11 and 12 prepare the patient for the task of becoming their own future therapists, which includes a discussion about relapse prevention. The homework focuses on strengthening confidence in healthy core beliefs and promoting self-acceptance and others-acceptance. Self-control techniques in difficult situations are practiced and solutions for possible relapses are tested before the end of the therapy.

Structurally, sessions 11–12 include:

- Prepare patient for the task of becoming their own future therapist;
- Discuss dependency problems and relapse prevention;
- Homework suggestions:
  - Continuing EFS-generated behavioral activation;
  - Continuous use of the self-control techniques in real-life situations.

References

Ellis, A., Dryden, W., & DiGiuseppe, R. (2007). *The practice of rational emotive behavior therapy*. New York, NY: Springer.

Giosan, C., Cobeanu, O., Mogoase, C., Muresan, V., Malta, L. S., Wyka, K., & Szentagotai, A. (2014). Evolutionary cognitive therapy versus standard cognitive therapy for depression: A protocol for a blinded, randomized, superiority clinical trial. *Trials, 15*(1), 83. https://doi.org/10.1186/1745-6215-15-83

Giosan, C., Muresan, V., & Moldovan, R. (2014). Cognitive evolutionary therapy for depression: A case study. *Clinical Case Reports, 2*(5), 228–236. https://doi.org/10.1002/ccr3.131

Irons, W. (1998). Adaptively relevant environments versus the environment of evolutionary adaptedness. *Evolutionary Anthropology: Issues, News, and Reviews, 6*(6), 194–204. https://doi.org/10.1002/(SICI)1520-6505(1998)6:6<194::AID-EVAN2>3.0.CO;2-B

Nesse, R. M., & Williams, G. C. (1994). *Why do we get sick? The new science of Darwinian medicine*. New York, NY: Times Books, Random House, Inc.

Appendices

Appendix 1: Nutrition

If necessary, the therapist should devise a nutritional plan for the patient, incorporating (some of) the foods our ancestors consumed during the times of our evolutionary history. Our ancestors' diet consisted primarily of fruits (e.g., apples, tomatoes, berries), non-starchy vegetables (e.g., cabbage, lettuce), nuts (e.g., hazelnuts, walnuts), occasional honey, and game meat (Cordain, 2011; Cordain et al., 2005). The typical pre-agricultural diet was virtually free of legumes (e.g., potatoes or beans), dairy products (e.g., milk or cheese) or grains (e.g., bread). The very little – if any – amounts of grains our ancestors consumed were in the form of sprouts, i.e., grains that could be eaten raw, uncooked. Our ancestors' vitamin intake was considerably higher than ours (Cordain, 2011; Cordain et al., 2005) and the meat our ancestors consumed had considerably lower amounts of saturated fat compared to farmed meat. The glycemic index of the typical foods our ancestors consumed was very low compared to the modern foods.

The evolutionary argument is that the fact that our ancestors lived for millions of years on this type of diet led to specific adaptations to these kinds of foods. In other words, time was too short since the discovery of agriculture 10,000 years ago for humans to have evolved adaptations to modern foods, such as diary or grains. This explains a multitude of ailments affecting humans today. One example is lactose intolerance, whose high prevalence in humans – up to 65% (NIH, n.d.) – is explained by the fact that our ancestors did not consume other animals' milk. Other examples are heart disease, diabetes, blood pressure, or cancer (Cordain, 2011).

While a direct link between diet and depression is yet not fully established, research documents strong links between a highly nutritious and balanced diet and health outcomes in general. As such, an evolutionary-driven intervention should include a nutritional component as described above.

C. Giosan, *Cognitive Evolutionary Therapy for Depression*, SpringerBriefs in Psychology, https://doi.org/10.1007/978-3-030-38874-4

Of course, compromises will have to be made in this regard, as not all patients will readily transition to a markedly different diet, and, in addition, some of the staple foods we consumed in our evolutionary past are hard to procure nowadays or might be allergens to some. For example, game will have to be replaced with low fat grocery-store meats, such as free-range turkey or organic chicken breast, as in countries such as US game commercialization is illegal. Wild berries will have to be replaced with foods that are available in grocery stores, preferably not very sweet, such as apples. White bread, which has the same glycemic index as glucose, can be replaced with nuts or with sprouted bread.

Appendix 2: Physical Activity

Our ancestors' lifestyle was very active compared to ours. They walked extensively in search for food (up to 20 miles per day), had to outrun predators, catch prey, or migrate frequently.

Ample research documents the benefits of physical activity on both mental and physical health (Eaton & Eaton, 2003). More specifically, physical activity has positive effects on depression, anxiety and self-esteem (Biddle & Asare, 2011; North, McCullagh, & Tran, 1990), as well as on general mental health (Clyne, 2001). People who engage in regular physical activity display more desirable health outcomes across a variety of physical conditions (Penedo & Dahn, 2005). Similarly, participants in randomized clinical trials of physical-activity interventions show better health outcomes, including better general and health-related quality of life, functional capacity and mood states (North et al., 1990; Penedo & Dahn, 2005). Several reviews suggest that even low doses of physical activity may be protective against depressive symptoms in children and adolescents (Biddle & Asare, 2011), adults (Teychenne, Ball, & Salmon, 2008), and the elderly (Palmer, 2005; Potter, Ellard, Rees, & Thorogood, 2011).

Contemporary humans engage in little physical exercise compared to the physically active lifestyle engaged in by ancestral hunter-gatherers (Cordain, Gotshall, & Eaton, 1997; Eaton & Eaton, 2003; Lima et al., 2008; O'Keefe & Cordain, 2004; Walker & Adam, 2003). Our ancestors would have gone through prolonged periods of sedentariness only following injuries, which provided the body cues to engage in life-preserving metabolic and stress related responses such as inflammation. In the modern societies, inflammatory responses are the cause of many chronic diseases, one explanation being the fact that contemporary humans are much more sedentary than our ancestors (Charansonney & Després, 2010).

References for Appendices

Biddle, S. J. H., & Asare, M. (2011). Physical Activity and Mental Health in Children and Adolescents: A Review of Reviews. *British Journal of Sports Medicine, 45*(11), 886–895. https://doi.org/10.1136/bjsports-2011-090185

Charansonney, O. L., & Després, J. P. (2010). Disease prevention—Should we target obesity or sedentary lifestyle? *Nature Reviews. Cardiology, 7*(8), 468–472. https://doi.org/10.1038/nrcardio.2010.68

Clyne, A. (2001). Physical Activity and Mental Health. *Physiotherapy, 87*(1), 49–50. https://doi.org/10.1016/S0031-9406(05)61195-9

Cordain, L. (2011). *The paleo diet: Lose weight and get healthy by eating the foods you were designed to eat* (Rev. ed.). Hoboken, NJ: Wiley.

Cordain, L., Gotshall, R. W., & Eaton, S. B. (1997). Evolutionary aspects of exercise. *World Review of Nutrition and Dietetics, 81*, 49–60.

Cordain, L., Eaton, S. B., Sebastian, A., Mann, N., Lindeberg, S., Watkins, B. A., … Brand-Miller, J. (2005). Origins and evolution of the Western diet: Health implications for the 21st century. *The American Journal of Clinical Nutrition, 81*(2), 341–354.

Eaton, S. B., & Eaton, S. B. (2003). An evolutionary perspective on human physical activity: Implications for health. *Comparative Biochemistry and Physiology. Part A, Molecular & Integrative Physiology, 136*(1), 153–159.

Lima, V. S., Iniguez, A. M., Otsuki, K., Ferreira, L. F., Araújo, A., Vicente, A. C. P., & Jansen, A. M. (2008). Chagas Disease in Ancient Hunter-Gatherer Population, Brazil. *Emerging Infectious Diseases, 14*(6), 1001–1002. https://doi.org/10.3201/eid1406.0707

NIH, G. H. (n.d.). *Lactose intolerance*. Retrieved February 18, 2018, from NIH.gov website: https://ghr.nlm.nih.gov/condition/lactose-intolerance

North, T. C., McCullagh, P., & Tran, Z. V. (1990). Effect of exercise on depression. *Exercise and Sport Sciences Reviews, 18*, 379–415.

O'Keefe, J. H., & Cordain, L. (2004). Cardiovascular disease resulting from a diet and lifestyle at odds with our Paleolithic genome: How to become a 21st-century hunter-gatherer. *Mayo Clinic Proceedings Mayo Clinic, 79*(1), 101–108.

Palmer, C. (2005). Exercise as a treatment for depression in elders. *Journal of the American Academy of Nurse Practitioners, 17*(2), 60–66. https://doi.org/10.1111/j.1041-2972.2005.00012.x

Penedo, F. J., & Dahn, J. R. (2005). Exercise and well-being: A review of mental and physical health benefits associated with physical activity. *Current Opinion in Psychiatry, 18*(2), 189–193.

Potter, R., Ellard, D., Rees, K., & Thorogood, M. (2011). A systematic review of the effects of physical activity on physical functioning, quality of life and depression in older people with dementia. *International Journal of Geriatric Psychiatry, 26*(10), 1000–1011. https://doi.org/10.1002/gps.2641

Teychenne, M., Ball, K., & Salmon, J. (2008). Physical activity and likelihood of depression in adults: A review. *Preventive Medicine, 46*(5), 397–411. https://doi.org/10.1016/j.ypmed.2008.01.009

Walker, B. F., & Adam, F. (2003). Nutrition, diet, physical activity, smoking, and longevity: From primitive hunter-gatherer to present passive consumer–how far can we go? *Nutrition Burbank Los Angeles County Calif, 19*(2), 169–173.

Index

C. Giosan, *Cognitive Evolutionary Therapy for Depression*, SpringerBriefs in Psychology, https://doi.org/10.1007/978-3-030-38874-4